SUNBEAMS
A BOOK OF QUOTATIONS

SUNBEAMS
A BOOK OF QUOTATIONS

edited
by

SY SAFRANSKY

North Atlantic Books
Berkeley, California

Sunbeams: A Book of Quotations

Copyright © 1990 by The Sun Publishing Company, Inc. No portion of this book, except for brief review, may be reproduced in any form without written permission of the publisher. For information, contact North Atlantic Books.

ISBN 1-55643-045-0

Published by North Atlantic Books
          P.O. Box 12327
          Berkeley, California 94712

This is issue #42 of the *Io* series.

Cover and book design by Paula Morrison
Typeset by Campaigne and Associates Typography
Printed in the United States of America.

Sunbeams: A Book of Quotations is sponsored by the Society for the Study of Native Arts and Sciences, a nonprofit educational corporation whose goals are to develop an educational and crosscultural perspective linking various scientific, social, and artistic fields; to nurture a holistic view of arts, sciences, humanities, and healing; and to publish and distribute literature on the relationship of mind, body, and nature.

INTRODUCTION

Once a month, my desk at *The Sun* becomes extravagantly cluttered with stacks of books and magazines and letters and scribbled notes. For hours, I sift through them—reading, jotting down a few words, staring out the window, reading some more, searching through hundreds of quotations for the handful that will become next month's Sunbeams.

It's a familiar ritual. But, even after all these years, I still don't know why I fall in love with some quotes and not others. Drawn from such diverse sources as stories, essays, speeches, interviews, novels, memoirs, and poems, the Sunbeams page surely reflects my own likes and dislikes, passions and confusions. Yet some strange alchemy seems to be at work: I can't be sure whether I choose Sunbeams or they choose me.

This is a collection of the best Sunbeams from more than a decade. Mercifully—for my sake and yours—I didn't try to organize the quotes into subjects; instead, they appear as they did in the magazine, with all the startling juxtapositions that honor, more accurately than any subject headings, the rich and paradoxical nature of our lives.

Placing certain quotations together is like seating strangers around a dinner table; you can't be sure where the conversation will lead. Also, it's amazing how often a quote will affect us in a way the author never could have imagined. Sometimes the meaning of a quote changes simply because it occurs out of context. But it's also true that certain words have a life of their own. Clear as a window, they allow us to see through them; reading them, we see what we need to see.

I haven't deliberately left out well-known quotations, though I tend to shy away from them. Certain favorite authors come up again and again, but if the same quote appears twice, it's in spite of the most rigorous proofreading. Every effort has been made to make sure the quotes are accurately worded and attributed; if the name of the work was known, it too was included. If a quote seemed worth using but, because of its gender-exclusive language, was plainly sexist, it appears unedited. Such a decision can be argued endlessly; I saw no choice but to be faithful to the original text.

Perhaps all anthologies owe a debt to kindred anthologies, and this one is no exception. I have more quote books than many small libraries; special favorites are Richard Kehl's *Silver Departures*, Art Spiegelman and Bob Schneider's *Whole Grains*, Russell McDougal's *Mirror Of Mind* and—yes—John Bartlett's *Familiar Quotations*, which I find surprisingly readable.

Thanks, finally, to all the readers of *The Sun* who have sent in suggestions for Sunbeams. and to everyone at *The Sun* who helped to prepare this book. If you'd like to know more about *The Sun*, an independent journal that publishes a wide range of essays interviews, fiction, and poetry—and still, every month, a page of Sunbeams—drop me a line at 107 North Roberson Street, Chapel Hill, NC 27516.

—Sy Safransky

Most quote books beg to be opened at random, but consider reading this book front to back. It's divided into "chapters" that correspond to the original Sunbeams pages from *The Sun*, set off from each other by ○ ○ ○ ○ ○ .

He who mounts a wild elephant goes where the wild elephant goes.

—Randolph Bourne

Properly, we shd. read for power. Man reading shd. be man intensely alive. The book shd. be a ball of light in one's hands.

—Ezra Pound

Since everything is but an apparition
Perfect in being what it is,
Having nothing to do with good or bad, acceptance or rejection,
One may well burst out in laughter.

—Longchenpa

When men dream, each has his own world. When they are awake, they have a common world.

—Heraclitus

Give light, and the darkness will disappear of itself.

—Desiderius Erasmus

The world's spiritual geniuses seem to discover universally that the mind's muddy river, this ceaseless flow of trivia and trash, cannot be dammed, and that trying to dam it is a waste of effort that might lead to madness.

—Annie Dillard

People talk about love as if it were something you could give, like an armful of flowers.

—Anne Morrow Lindbergh

Prayer is not the moment when God and humans are in relationship, for that is always. Prayer is taking initiative to intentionally respond to God's presence.

—L. Robert Keck

Prayers are answered in the way they're asked.

—Ram Tirth

I felt it better to speak to God than about Him.

—St. Theresa of Lisieux

1

I looked more widely around me, I studied the lives of the masses of humanity, and I saw that, not two or three, or ten, but hundreds, thousands, millions, had so understood the meaning of life that they were able both to live and to die. All these men were well acquainted with the meaning of life and death, quietly labored, endured privation and suffering, lived and died, and saw in all this, not a vain, but a good thing.

—Leo Tolstoy

Whenever you get there, there's no there there.
—Gertrude Stein

○ ○ ○ ○ ○

After fifteen years of total solitude, St. Seraphim of Sarow exclaimed at the sight of the least visitor, "Oh joy!" Would one who had never refrained from rubbing shoulders with his fellow men have dared to greet them in such an extravagant fashion?

—E.M. Cioran

After ecstasy, the laundry.
—Zen saying

I wouldn't write a book to win a fight. I'd rather go fifteen rounds with Sonny Liston. At least it would be over in an hour and I could go to bed. But a book takes me two years, if I'm lucky. Eight hours a day, seven days a week, 365 days a year, that's the only way I know how to do it. You have to sit alone in a room with only a tree out the window to talk to. You have to sit there

churning out draft after draft of crap, waiting like a neglected baby for just one drop of mother's milk.

—Philip Roth

A writer is someone for whom writing is more difficult than it is for other people.
—Thomas Mann

One must learn to love, and go through a good deal of suffering to get to it, like any knight of the grail, and the journey is always toward the other soul, not away from it. Do you think that love is an accomplished thing, the day it is recognized? It isn't. To love, you have to learn to understand the other more than she understands herself, and to submit to her understanding of you. It is damnably difficult and painful, but it is the only thing which endures. You mustn't think that your desire or your fundamental need is to make a career, or to fill up your life with activity, or even provide for your family materially. It isn't. Your most vital necessity in life is that you shall love your wife completely and implicitly and in entire nakedness of body and spirit. Then you will have peace and inner security no matter how many things go wrong. And this peace and security will leave you free to act and to produce your own work, a real and independent workman.

—D.H. Lawrence

There are so many little dyings every day, it doesn't matter which one of them is death.
—Kenneth Patchen

Our own heart always exceeds us.
—Rainer Maria Rilke

To confront a person with his own shadow is to show him his own light.

—Carl Jung

Now all my teachers are dead except silence.

—W.S. Merwin

I have died so little today, friend, forgive me.

—Thomas Lux

All paths are the same: they lead nowhere. . . . They are paths going through the bush, or into the bush. In my own life I could say I have traversed long, long paths but I am not anywhere. My benefactor's question has meaning now. Does this path have a heart? If it does, the path is good; if it doesn't, it is of no use. Both paths lead nowhere; but one has a heart, the other doesn't. One makes for a joyful journey; as long as you follow it, you are one with it. The other will make you curse your life. One makes you strong; the other weakens you.

—Carlos Castaneda
The Teachings Of Don Juan

When there is no desire to satisfy yourself, there is no aggression or speed. . . . Because there is no rush to achieve, you can afford to relax. Because you can afford to relax, you can afford to keep company with yourself, you can afford to make love with yourself, to be friends with yourself.

—Chögyam Trungpa
Cutting Through Spiritual Materialism

In constantly seeking to actualize your ideal, you will have no time for composure. But if you are always prepared for accepting everything we see as something appearing from nothing . . . then at that moment you will have perfect composure.

—Suzuki Roshi
Zen Mind, Beginner's Mind

That life is worth living is the most necessary of assumptions, and were it not assumed, the most impossible of conclusions.

—George Santayana

You try being alone, without any form of distraction, and you will see how quickly you want to get away from yourself and forget what you are. That is why this enormous structure of professional amusement, of automated distraction, is so prominent a part of what we call civilization. If you observe, you will see that people the world over are becoming more and more distracted, increasingly sophisticated and worldly. The multiplication of pleasures, the innumerable books that are being published, the newspaper pages filled with sporting events—surely, all these indicate that we constantly want to be amused. Because we are inwardly empty, dull, mediocre, we use our relationships and our social reforms as a means of escaping from ourselves. I wonder if you have noticed how lonely most people are? And to escape from loneliness we run to temples, churches, or mosques, we dress up and attend social functions, we watch television, listen to the radio, read, and so on. . . . If you inquire a little into boredom you will find that the cause of it is loneliness. It is in order to escape from loneliness that we want to be

together, we want to be entertained, to have distractions of every kind: gurus, religious ceremonies, prayers, or the latest novel. Being inwardly lonely we become mere spectators in life; and we can be the players only when we understand loneliness and go beyond it.

. . . because beyond it lies the real treasure.

—J. Krishnamurti
Think On These Things

○ ○ ○ ○ ○

Whenever you hear anyone talking about a cultural or even about a human problem, you should never forget to inquire who the speaker really is. The more general the problem, the more he will smuggle his own personal psychology into the account he gives of it.

—Carl Jung

Pay attention to minute particulars. Take care of the little ones. Generalization and abstraction are the plea of the hypocrite, scoundrel, and knave.

—William Blake

I think there are some clues as to what makes us willing to murder in the name of truth.

One is our desire to possess truth, rather than serve it. I am increasingly convinced that the need to be right has nothing whatsoever to do with the love of truth. But to face the implications of this means accepting a painful inner emptiness: I am not now what I sense, some-

how, I am meant to be. I do not know what I feel from the bottom of my heart; I need to know. The beginning of wisdom is not to flee from this condition or distract yourself from it; it is essential not to fill it up with answers which have not been earned. It is important . . . to learn how to wait, with empty hands. It is the desire to fill up that emptiness which leads to political or religious fanaticism. By possessing the truth (which is very different from being possessed by it) you anchor yourself—the big hollow winds, the self-doubts are silenced. It is the truths arrived at this way which men kill for.

—John Garvey

The search for truth is but the honest searching out of everything that interferes with truth. Truth *is*. It can neither be lost nor sought nor found. It is there, wherever you are, being within you. Yet it can be recognized or unrecognized.

—*A Course In Miracles*

All our understanding of the abstractions of philosophy is like a single hair in the vastness of space.

—Master Tokusan

The thing is not to cling to thoughts but to let them go. By letting them go, they are replaced by other thoughts until you become aware of thought following thought. As the immortal bard, Shakespeare, said at the end of the last play, *The Tempest*, when Prospero goes home, having burned his magic books of ego and thrown away his magic wand of power, "to Milan [I'll go] where every third thought shall be my grave." You become aware of your thoughts in that sense. Shakespeare was aware that there's one thought, and then there's another thought, and then there's another thought, and then there's another thought, and there's a space in between. So you become aware of the mind thinking and the thoughts passing through. That gives you a profile on your thoughts, so to speak. Not that you have to think of them, or inspect them, or grab them by the tail. You become aware that all those thoughts are passing through your mind. You look at them from the outside almost. You become the observer of your own mind, which is useful for an artist.

—Allen Ginsberg

Great geniuses have the shortest biographies.
—Ralph Waldo Emerson

Some people always sigh in thanking God.
—Elizabeth Barrett Browning

In my hunt for the secret of life, I started my research in histology. Unsatisfied by the information that cellular morphology could give me about life, I turned to physiology. Finding physiology too complex I took up pharmacology. Still finding the situation too complicated I turned to bacteriology. But bacteria were even too complex, so I descended to the molecular level, studying chemistry and physical chemistry. After twenty years' work, I was led to conclude that to understand life we have to descend to the electronic level, and to the world of wave mechanics. But electrons are just electrons, and have no life at all. Evidently on the way I lost life; it had run out between my fingers.

—Albert Szent-Gyorgyi
Personal Reminiscences

One day while studying a Yeats poem I decided to write poetry the rest of my life. I recognized that a single short poem has room for history, music, psychology, religious thought, mood, occult speculation, character, and events of one's own life. I still feel surprised that such various substances can find shelter and nourishment in a poem. A poem in fact may be a sort of nourishing liquid, such as one uses to keep an amoeba alive. If prepared right, a poem can keep an image or a thought or insights on history or the psyche alive for years, as well as our desires and airy impulses.

—Robert Bly

Time is nature's way of preventing everything from happening at once.

—Graffiti

○ ○ ○ ○ ○

Our lives are like islands in the sea, or like trees in the forest, which co-mingle their roots in the darkness underground.

—William James

Let my hidden weeping arise and blossom.
—Rainer Maria Rilke

The dangerous aspects of nature that kept our forebears watchful and humble have now almost disappeared outside; but they have turned inward (wilderness without—wilderness within!) so that the whole of Western society rapidly approaches the physical and mental cracking point from the inner dangers alone. This is no joking matter, for should the outer wilderness disappear altogether, it would inevitably resurrect powerfully from within, whereupon it would immediately be projected. Enemies would be created, and its terrifying aspects would take revenge for our neglect, our lack of reverence, our ruthless interference with that beautiful order of things.

—C.A. Meier

A language is a map of our failures.

—Adrienne Rich

In a city a man may feel second to none. But alone in the immensity of the universe, among all the creatures that preceded man and built up the human species, even a most fervent atheist will wonder if Darwin found the visible road but not the invisible mechanism.

—Thor Heyerdahl
The Tigris Expedition

"Take my own father! You know what he said in his last moments? On his deathbed, he defied me to name a man who had enjoyed a better life. In spite of the dreadful pain, his face *radiated* happiness," said Mother, nodding her head comfortably. "Happiness drives out pain, as fire burns out fire."

—Mary Lavin

Love that stammers, that stutters, is apt to be the love that loves best.

—Gabriela Mistral

The erotic instinct is something questionable, and will always be so whatever a future set of laws may have to say on the matter. It belongs, on the one hand, to the original animal nature of man, which will exist as long as man has an animal body. On the other hand, it is connected with the highest forms of the spirit. But it blooms only when spirit and instinct are in true harmony. If one or the other aspect is missing, then an injury occurs, or at least there is a one-sided lack of balance which easily slips into the pathological. Too much of the animal disfigures the civilized human being, too much culture makes a sick animal.

—Carl Jung
The Psychology Of The Unconscious

Can one ever remember love? It's like trying to summon up the smell of roses in a cellar. You might see a rose, but never the perfume.

—Arthur Miller
After The Fall

It occurred to him (not for the first time) that the world was divided sharply down the middle: some lived careful lives and some lived careless lives, and everything that happened could be explained by the difference between them. But he could not have said, not in a million years, why he was so moved by the sight of Muriel's thin quilt trailing across the floor where she must have dragged it when she rose in the morning.

—Anne Tyler
The Accidental Tourist

Von Neumann lived in this elegant house in Princeton. As I parked my car and walked in, there was this very large Great Dane dog bouncing around on the front lawn. I knocked on the door and von Neumann, who was a small, quiet, modest kind of man, came to the door and bowed to me and said, "Bigelow, won't you come in," and so forth, and this dog brushed between our legs and went into the living room. He proceeded to lie down on the rug in front of everybody, and we had the entire interview—whether I would come, what I knew, what the job was going to be like—and this lasted maybe forty minutes, with the dog wandering all around the house. Toward the end of it, von Neumann asked me if I always traveled with the dog. But of course it wasn't my dog, and it wasn't his either, but von Neumann—being a diplomatic, middle-European person—kindly avoided mentioning it until the end.

—Julian Bigelow
Ed Regis's *Who Got Einstein's Office?*

○ ○ ○ ○ ○

There are never enough "I love you"s.
—Lenny Bruce

People are like stained-glass windows. They sparkle and shine when the sun is out, but when the darkness sets in, their true beauty is revealed only if there is a light from within.
—Elisabeth Kübler-Ross

A thankful person is thankful under all circumstances. A complaining soul complains even if he lives in paradise.
—Baha'u'llah

To you I'm an atheist. To God I'm the loyal opposition.
—Woody Allen

You can plan events, but if they go according to your plan they are not events.
—John Berger

If I could only remember that the days were not bricks to be laid row on row, to be built into a solid house, where one might dwell in safety and peace, but only food for the fires of the heart.
—Edmund Wilson

Burn all the maps to your body.
—Richard Brautigan

The next message you need is always right where you are.
—Ram Dass

I really think I write about everyday life. I don't think I'm quite as odd as others say I am. Life is intrinsically, well, boring and dangerous at the same time. At any given moment the floor may open up. Of course, it almost never does; that's what makes it so boring.
—Edward Gorey

There wouldn't be such a thing as counterfeit gold if there were no real gold somewhere.
—Sufi proverb

Your task is not to seek for love, but merely to seek and find all of the barriers within yourself that you have built against it.
—*A Course In Miracles*

Who has not sat before his own heart's curtain? It lifts: and the scenery is falling apart.
—Rainer Maria Rilke

Close one sad eye. Yes. Close the other sad eye. Yes. I can see now.

—Yehuda Amichai

○ ○ ○ ○ ○

It is only necessary to know that love is a direction and not a state of the soul. If one is unaware of this, one falls into despair at the first onslaught of affliction.

—Simone Weil

Take long walks in stormy weather or through deep snow in the fields and woods, if you would keep your spirits up. Deal with brute nature. Be cold and hungry and weary.

—Henry David Thoreau

It always strikes me and it is very peculiar that when we see the image of indescribable and unutterable desolation—of loneliness, poverty, and misery, the end of all things, or their extreme—then rises in our mind the thought of God.

—Vincent van Gogh

Knowing who in fact one is, being conscious of the universal and impersonal life that lives itself through each of us, that's the art of living, and that's what one can help the dying to go on practicing.

—Aldous Huxley

An intelligent man cannot become anything seriously, and it is only the fool who becomes anything.

—Fyodor Dostoyevsky

I am always between two worlds, always in conflict. I would like sometimes to rest, to be at peace, to choose a nook, make a final choice, but I can't. Some nameless, undescribable fear and anxiety keeps me on the move. On certain evenings like this I would like to feel whole. Only half of me is sitting by the fire. Only my hands are sewing.

—Anaïs Nin

A man doesn't learn to understand anything unless he loves it.

—Johann Wolfgang von Goethe

You can think as much as you like but you will invent nothing better than bread and salt.

—Russian proverb

God is love. His plan for creation can only be rooted in love. Does not that simple thought, rather than erudite reasonings, offer solace to the human heart?

—Paramahansa Yogananda

Perhaps the efforts of the true poets, founders, religions, literatures, all ages, have been, and ever will be, our time and times to come, essentially the same—to bring people back from their present strayings and sickly abstractions, to the costless, average, divine, original concrete.

—Walt Whitman

A change in the weather is enough to renew the world and ourselves.

—Marcel Proust

It does not astonish or make us angry that it takes a whole year to bring into the house three great white peonies and two pale blue iris. It seems altogether right and appropriate that these glories are earned with long patience and faith, . . . and also that it is altogether right and appropriate that they cannot last. Yet in our human relations we are outraged when the supreme moments, the moments of flowering, must be waited for . . . and then cannot *last*. We reach a summit, and then have to go down again.

—May Sarton

○ ○ ○ ○ ○

Question: What is the cause of the world?
Answer: Love.
Question: Why do men revolt?
Answer: To find beauty, either in life or in death.
Question: What for each of us is inevitable?
Answer: Happiness.
Question: And what is the greatest marvel?
Answer: Each day, death strikes, and we live as though we were immortal. This is the greatest marvel.

—*The Mahabharata*

Seek not to follow in the footsteps of men of old; seek what they sought.

—Matsuo Basho

I am against revolutions because they always involve a return to the status quo. I am against the status quo both *before* and *after* revolutions. I don't want to wear a black shirt or a red shirt. I want to wear the shirt that suits my taste. And I don't want to salute like an automaton either.

I prefer to shake hands when I meet someone I like. The fact is, to put it simply, I am positively against all this crap which is carried on first in the name of this thing, then in the name of that. I believe only in what is active, immediate, and personal.

—Henry Miller

You do not have to sit outside in the dark. If, however, you want to look at the stars, you will find that darkness is necessary. But the stars neither require nor demand it.

—Annie Dillard

Despair is the price one pays for setting oneself an impossible aim. It is, one is told, the unforgivable sin, but it is the sin the corrupt or evil man never practices. He always has hope. He never reaches the freezing point of knowing absolute failure. Only the man of goodwill car-

 **SUNBEAMS**

ries always in his heart this capacity for damnation.

—Graham Greene
The Heart Of The Matter

A wonderful fact to reflect upon, that every human creature is constituted to be that profound secret and mystery to every other. A solemn consideration, when I enter a great city by night, that every one of those darkly clustered houses encloses its own secret; that every room in every one of them encloses its own secret; that every beating heart in the thousands of breasts there is, in some of its imaginings, a secret to the heart nearest it.

—Charles Dickens

You can't eat language but it eases thirst.

—Bernard Malamud

Terry Gross: Can you share some of your favorite comments from readers that you've gotten over the years?

Maurice Sendak: Oh, there's so many. Can I give you just one that I really like? It was from a little boy. He sent me a charming card with a little drawing. I loved it. I answer all my children's letters—sometimes very hastily—but this one I lingered over. I sent him a postcard and I drew a picture of a Wild Thing on it. I wrote, "Dear Jim, I loved your card." Then I got a letter back from his mother and she said, "Jim loved your card so much he ate it." That to me was one of the highest compliments I've ever received. He didn't care that it was an original drawing or anything. He saw it, he loved it, he ate it.

—*Applause* magazine

Rule Number 1 is, don't sweat the small stuff. Rule Number 2 is, it's all small stuff.

—Robert Eliot

Believing ourselves to be possessors of absolute truth degrades us: we regard every person whose way of thinking is different from ours as a monster and a threat and by so doing turn our own selves into monsters and threats to our fellows.

—Octavio Paz

. . . And love, what is love but
that dark reflecting lake that any creature
may have the good or ill fortune to glance into.

—Stephen Dobyns

Our lives will be changed. Both our beliefs and our actions will become more responsive to God's spirit. But this will happen only as we allow ourselves to be engulfed by contradictions which God alone can resolve. With Jonah, we will be delivered. But first, we will be swallowed into darkness.

—Parker J. Palmer

What's holding her back
drives her on. . . .

—Osip Mandelstam

○ ○ ○ ○ ○

What does "car" mean? A car in a showroom, a car heading straight toward me, a car needing constant repair, all have such isolated meanings that the name "car" cannot be said to stand for any one thing. That too is true of Scott or John or Gayle. God is in them only when God is in my mind. Only love can see steadily, consistently. Love makes one thing of all that it sees.

—Hugh Prather
There Is A Place Where You Are Not Alone

Something we were withholding made us weak
Until we found it was ourselves.

—Robert Frost

There is only one good definition of God: the freedom that allows other freedoms to exist.

—John Fowles
The French Lieutenant's Woman

As Albert Einstein once said to me: "Two things are infinite: the universe and human stupidity." But what is much more widespread than the actual stupidity is the *playing* stupid, turning off your ear, not listening, not seeing . . . playing helpless.

—Fritz Perls
Gestalt Therapy Verbatim

I am plagued by doubts. What if everything is an illusion and nothing exists? In that case, I definitely overpaid for my carpet. If only God would give me some clear sign! Like making a large deposit in my name at a Swiss bank.

—Woody Allen
Without Feathers

The experience of oneself relating to other things is actually a momentary discrimination, a fleeting thought. If we generate these fleeting thoughts fast enough, we can create the illusion of continuity and solidity. It is like watching a movie; the individual film frames are played so quickly that they generate the illusion of continual movement. So we build up an idea, a preconception, that self and other are solid and continuous. And once we have this idea, we manipulate our thoughts to confirm it, and are afraid of any contrary evidence. It is this fear of exposure, this denial of impermanence, that imprisons us. It is only by acknowledging impermanence that there is the chance to die and the space to be reborn and the possibility of appreciating life as a creative process.

—Chögyam Trungpa
The Myth Of Freedom

It is the same when Siddhartha has an aim, a goal. Siddhartha does nothing; he waits, he thinks, he fasts, but he goes through the affairs of the world like the stone through the water, without doing anything, without bestirring himself; he is drawn and lets himself fall.

—Hermann Hesse
Siddhartha

You thought, as a boy, that a mage is one who can do anything. So I thought, once. So did we all. And the truth is that as a man's real power grows and his knowledge widens, ever the way he can follow grows narrower: until at last he chooses nothing, but does only and wholly what he *must do*.

—Ursula K. LeGuin
A Wizard Of Earthsea

One of the pleasures of middle age is to find out that one *was* right, and that one was much righter than one knew at, say, seventeen or twenty-three.

—Ezra Pound

But is work something that we have a right to escape? And can we escape it with impunity? We are probably the first entire people ever to think so. All the ancient wisdom that has come down to us counsels otherwise. It tells us that work is necessary to us, as much a part of our condition as mortality; that good work is our salvation and our joy; that shoddy or dishonest or self-serving work is our curse and our doom. We have tried to escape the sweat and sorrow promised in Genesis—only to find that, in order to do so, we must forswear love and excellence, health and joy.

—Wendell Berry
The Unsettling Of America

 Why are you unhappy?
Because 99.9 per cent
Of everything you do
Is for yourself—
And there isn't one.

—Wei Wu Wei

The best thing about the future is that it only comes one day at a time.

—Abraham Lincoln

○ ○ ○ ○ ○

Time is Breath.

—G.I. Gurdjieff

The morning glory which blooms for an hour
Differs not at heart from the giant pine,
Which lives for a thousand years.

—Zen poem

Time is an illusion perpetrated by the manufacturers of space.

—Graffiti

There is only the moment, and yet the moment is always giving way to the next, so that there is not even Now, there is Nothing. True, true. There is Nothing, if that is the way to understand how much there is.

—M.C. Richards
Centering

Tomorrow is the most important thing in life. Comes to us at midnight very clean. It's perfect when it arrives and puts itself in our hands. It hopes we've learned something from yesterday.

—John Wayne

. . . translucent time is closing up its moments
and ripens inwards, throwing out its roots,
it grows within me, occupies me wholly,
its foliage flings me out deliriously. . . .

—Octavio Paz

For if we open our eyes and see clearly, it becomes obvious that there is no other time than this instant, and that the past and the future are abstractions without any concrete reality. Until this has become clear, it seems that our life is all past and future, and that the present is nothing more than the infinitesimal hairline which divides them. From this comes the sensation of "having no time," of a world which hurries by so rapidly that it is gone before we can enjoy it. But through "awakening to the instant" one sees that this is the reverse of the truth: it is rather the past and future which are the fleeting illusions, and the present which is eternally real.

—Alan Watts
The Way Of Zen

Time is what keeps the light from reaching us. There is no greater obstacle to God than time. And not only time but temporalities, not only temporal things but temporal affections; not only temporal affections but the very taint and smell of time.

—Meister Eckhart

You are not stuck in time like a fly in a closed bottle, whose wings are therefore useless. You cannot trust your physical senses to give you a true picture of reality. They are lovely liars, with such a fantastic tale to tell that you believe it without question.

—Seth
Jane Roberts' *Seth Speaks*

○ ○ ○ ○ ○

Suppose someone were to say, "Imagine this butterfly exactly as it is, but ugly instead of beautiful."

—Ludwig Wittgenstein

In language we have to try to balance the extreme particularity of our unique personal experience and the generality of human experience. Vital speech involves a balancing of both concerns. Personal experience, one's particular experience, if it doesn't seek its place in the gen-

eral human experience, is incommunicable. And general human experience, if it isn't felt in the terms of particular experience, is virtually incommunicable, too, and, moreover, tyrannical.

—Wendell Berry

Put down your opinion, your condition, your situation, then you will not be stuck. Always stay open. Working in a gas station will be no problem, or cleaning someone's house. If you are holding your idea, "I want a high-class job, or a house, or a car," then you will have a problem. Zen means put everything down. Then you can control any situation or condition.

—Seung Sahn

I judge as the sunlight judges, falling upon a helpless thing.

—Walt Whitman

Be happy. It's one way of being wise.

—Colette

Your health is bound to be affected if, day after day, you say the opposite of what you feel, if you grovel before what you dislike and rejoice at what brings you nothing but misfortune. Our nervous system isn't just a fiction; it's a part of our physical body, and our soul exists in space, and is inside us, like the teeth in our mouth. It can't be forever violated with impunity.

—Boris Pasternak

You walk on carrying on your shoulders a glass door to some house that's not been found. There's no handle. You can't insure it. Can't put it down.

—W.S. Merwin

13

Sleep faster. We need the pillows.

—Yiddish proverb

One must not cheat anybody, not even the world of its triumph.

—Franz Kafka

Love winter when the plant says nothing.

—Thomas Merton

Where did the truth go? The key was mislaid in an army of doors, it was there on its ring with the others, but the lock is nowhere in the world. No world for the key to get lost in, no true or false, in the end.

—Pablo Neruda

All the arts we practice are apprenticeship. The big art is our life.

—M.C. Richards

For example, everyone automatically assumes that the present is the result of the past. Turn it around, and consider whether the past may not be a result of the present. The past may be streaming back from the now, like the country as seen from an airplane.

—Alan Watts

When they tell you to grow up, they mean stop growing.

—Tom Robbins

○ ○ ○ ○ ○

There is a great man who makes every man feel small. But the real great man is the man who makes every man feel great.

—G.K. Chesterton

When the stomach is full, it is easy to talk of fasting.

—St. Jerome

Treat the other man's faith gently; it is all he has to believe with. His mind was created for his own thoughts, not yours or mine.

—Henry S. Haskins

God gives the nuts, but he does not crack them.

—German proverb

It is only by feeling your love that the poor will forgive you for the gifts of bread.

—St. Vincent de Paul

Seldom, or perhaps never, does a marriage develop into an individual relationship smoothly and without crises; there is no coming to consciousness without pain.

—Carl Jung

A tree growing out of the ground is as wonderful today as it ever was. It does not need to adopt new and startling methods.

—Robert Henri

The world is God's language to us.

—Simone Weil

Our business is to wake up. We have to find ways in which to detect the whole of reality in the one illusory part which our self-centered consciousness permits us to see. We must not live thoughtlessly, taking our illusion for the complete reality, but at the same time we must not live too thoughtfully in the sense of trying to escape from the dream state. We must be continuously on our watch for ways in which we may enlarge our consciousness.

—Aldous Huxley

Rose-colored glasses are never made in bifocals. Nobody wants to read the small print in dreams.

—Ann Landers

The idea of a meaningless universe is in itself a highly creative imaginative act. Animals . . . could not imagine such an idiocy, so the theory shows an incredible accomplishment of an obviously ordered mind and intellect that can *imagine* itself to be the result of non-order or chaos—you have a creature who is capable of mapping its own brain, imagining that the brain's fantastic regulated order could emerge from a reality that has no meaning.

—Seth
Jane Roberts' *The Individual And
The Nature Of Mass Events*

I do not sit down at my desk to put into verse something that is already clear in my mind. If it were clear in my mind, I should have no incentive or need to write about it. . . . We do not write in order to be understood; we write in order to understand.

—C. Day Lewis
The Poetic Image

True myth may serve for thousands of years as an inexhaustible source of intellectual specula-

tion, religious joy, ethical inquiry, and artistic renewal. The real mystery is not destroyed by reason. The fake one is. You look at it and it vanishes. You look at the Blond Hero—really look—and he turns into a gerbil. But you look at Apollo, and he looks back at you. The poet Rilke looked at a statue of Apollo about fifty years ago, and Apollo spoke to him. "You must change your life," he said. When the true myth rises into consciousness, that is always its message. You must change your life.

—Ursula K. LeGuin

Can a mortal ask questions which God finds unanswerable? Quite easily, I should think. All nonsense questions are unanswerable. How many hours are there in a mile? Is yellow square or round? Probably half the questions we ask—half our great theological and metaphysical problems—are like that.

—C.S. Lewis
A Grief Observed

○ ○ ○ ○ ○

The most exhausting thing in my life is being insincere.

—Anne Morrow Lindbergh

Words hang like wash on the line, blowing in the winds of the mind.

—Rameshwar Das

Everyone wants to understand painting. Why don't they try to understand the song of the birds? Why do they love a night, a flower, every-

thing which surrounds man, without attempting to understand them? Whereas where painting is concerned, they want to understand.

—Pablo Picasso

"Thou shalt love the Lord thy God with thy whole heart, with thy whole soul, and with thy whole mind." This is the commandment of the great God, and He cannot command the impossible. Love is a fruit in season at all times, and within reach of every hand. Anyone may gather it and no limit is set. Everyone can reach this love through meditation, spirit of prayer, and sacrifice, by an intense inner life.

—Mother Theresa

Nothing real can be threatened. Nothing unreal exists.

—*A Course In Miracles*

Truth is completely spontaneous. Lies have to be taught.

—R. Buckminster Fuller

We use the word "love" but we have no more understanding of love than we do of anger or fear or jealousy or even joy, because we have seldom investigated what that state of mind is. What are the feelings we so quickly label as love? For many what is called love is not lovely at all but is a tangle of needs and desires, of momentary ecstasies and bewilderment. Moments of unity, of intense feelings of closeness, occur in a mind so fragile that the least squint or sideways glance shatters its oneness into a dozen ghostly paranoias. When we say love we usually mean some emotion, some deep feeling for an object or person, that momentar-

ily allows us to open to another. But in such emotional love, self-protection is never very far away. Still there is "business" to the relationship: clouds of jealousy, possessiveness, guilt, intentional and unintentional manipulation, separateness, and the shadow of all previous "loves" darken the light of oneness. But what I mean by love is not an emotion, it is a state of being. True love has no object. Many speak of their unconditional love for another. Unconditional love is the experience of being; there is no "I" and "other," and anyone or anything it touches is experienced in love. You cannot unconditionally love someone. You can only *be* unconditional love. It is not a dualistic emotion. It is a sense of oneness with all that is. The experience of love arises when we surrender our separateness into the universal. It is a feeling of unity. You don't love another, you *are* another. There is no fear because there is no separation.

—Stephen Levine
Who Dies?

Each small task of everyday life is part of the total harmony of the universe.

—St. Theresa of Lisieux

Yes, it is better to look from the window than not to look at all, but to look through the window cannot be compared to the windowless sky.

—Bhagwan Shree Rajneesh

I do not know what I may appear to the world, but to myself I seem to have been only a child playing on the seashore while the great ocean of truth lay all undiscovered before me.

—Sir Isaac Newton

The hidden harmony is stronger than the visible.

—Heraclitus

Be like the bird, pausing in his flight
On limb too slight,
Feels it give way, yet sings,
Knowing he has wings.

—Victor Hugo

We turn to God for help when our foundations are shaking, only to learn that it is God who is shaking them.

—Charles C. West

○ ○ ○ ○ ○

We have to be utterly broken before we can realize that it is impossible to better the truth. It is the truth that we deny which so tenderly and forgivingly picks up the fragments and puts them together again.

—Laurens Van der Post

In later life I care only for peace;
Affairs of state are none of my concern.
I know I have no plan to save the world,
Only my old retreat here in this world.
My girdle loosened to the cool pine wind,
I play the lute beneath the mountain moon.
You ask the laws of failure and success?
The fishermen are singing in the cove. . . .

—Chinese poem

There is a field where all wonderful perfections of microscope and telescope fail. All exquisite niceties of weights and measures as well as that which is behind them, the keen and driving power of the mind. No facts, however indubitably detected, no effort of reason, however magnificently maintained, can prove that Bach's music is beautiful.

—Edith Hamilton

The hammer is the abstraction of each one of its hammerings.

—José Ortega y Gasset

It is easier to fight for one's principles than to live up to them.

—Alfred Adler

Husband and wife are like the two equal parts of a soybean. If the two parts are put under the earth separately, they will not grow. The soybean will grow only when the parts are covered by the skin. Marriage is the skin which covers each of them and makes them one.

—Hari Dass

Be wary of any enterprise that requires new clothes.

—Henry David Thoreau

The test of a first-rate intelligence is the ability to hold two opposed ideas in the mind at the same time, and still retain the ability to function.

—F. Scott Fitzgerald

Oh, you who are trying to learn the marvel of Love through the copy book of reason, I'm very much afraid that you will never really see the point.

—Hafiz of Shiraz

With love, even the rocks will open.
— Hazrat Inayat Khan

○ ○ ○ ○ ○

The poor long for riches and the rich for heaven, but the wise long for a state of tranquility.
— Swami Rama

This comes up all the time in mechanical work. A hang-up. You just sit and stare and think, and search randomly for new information, and go away and come back again, and after a while the unseen factors start to emerge.
— Robert M. Pirsig
Zen And The Art Of Motorcycle Maintenance

A woman can't be, until a girl dies. . . . I mean the sprites that girls are, so different from us, all their fancies, their illusions, their flower world, the dreams they live in.
— Christina Stead

It saddens me to become once again an independent woman. It was a deep joy to depend on his insight and guidance.
— Anaïs Nin

For a small reward a man will hurry away on a long journey, while for eternal life many will hardly take a single step.
— Thomas à Kempis

Frugality is one of the most beautiful and joyful words in the English language, and yet it is one that we are culturally cut off from understand-ing and enjoying. The consumption society has made us feel that happiness lies in having things, and has failed to teach us the happiness of not having things.
— Elise Boulding

It is life near the bone where it is sweetest.
— Henry David Thoreau
Walden

We say that we cannot bear our troubles but when we get to them we bear them.
— Ning Lao T'ai-t'ai

But this dark is deep:
now I warm you with my blood, listen
to this flesh.
It is far truer than poems.
— Marina Tsvetayeva

God gives food to every bird, but does not throw it into the nest.
— Montenegrin proverb

A man must have aunts and cousins, must buy carrots and turnips, must have barn and woodshed, must go to market and to the blacksmith's shop, must saunter and sleep and be inferior and silly.
— Ralph Waldo Emerson

Plants bear witness to the reality of roots.
— Moses Maimonides

She had been so wicked that in all her life she had done only one good deed—given an onion to a beggar. So she went to hell. As she lay in torment she saw the onion, lowered down from

heaven by an angel. She caught hold of it. He began to pull her up. The other damned saw what was happening and caught hold of it too. She was indignant and cried, "Let go—it's my onion," and as soon as she said, "My onion," the stalk broke and she fell back into the flames.

—E.M. Forster
The Hill Of Devi

The empiricist . . . thinks he believes only what he sees, but he is much better at believing than at seeing.

—George Santayana

What we give to the poor for Christ's sake is what we carry with us when we die.

—Peter Marin

We who lived in concentration camps can remember the men who walked through the huts comforting others, giving away their last piece of bread. They may have been few in number, but they offer sufficient proof that everything can be taken away from a man but one thing: the last of the human freedoms—to choose one's attitude in any given set of circumstances, to choose one's own way.

—Viktor Frankl

○ ○ ○ ○ ○

All truly wise thoughts have been thought already thousands of times; but to make them truly ours, we must think them over again honestly, till they take root in our personal experience.

—Johann Wolfgang von Goethe

You must understand the whole of life, not just one little part of it. That is why you must read, that is why you must look at the skies, that is why you must sing, and dance, and write poems, and suffer, and understand, for all that is life.

—J. Krishnamurti
Think On These Things

If we could read the secret history of our enemies, we would find in each man's life a sorrow and a suffering enough to disarm all hostility.

—Henry Wadsworth Longfellow

It matters immensely. The slightest sound matters. The most momentary rhythm matters. You can do as you please, yet everything matters.

—Wallace Stevens

The composer Stravinsky had written a new piece with a difficult violin passage. After it had been in rehearsal for several weeks, the solo

violinist came to Stravinsky and said he was sorry, he had tried his best, the passage was too difficult, no violinist could play it. Stravinsky said, "I understand that. What I am after is the sound of someone trying to play it."

—Thomas Powers

All mankind is divided into three classes: those that are immovable, those that are movable, and those that move.

—Arabian proverb

Burke is not affected by the reality of distress touching his heart, but by the showy resemblance of it striking his imagination. He pities the plumage, but forgets the dying bird.

—Thomas Paine

Nobody realizes that some people expend tremendous energy merely to be normal.

—Albert Camus

Psychology is nothing but a history which persists in us because we have not been able to rise from it.

—Joel Kovel

Don't wait for some miracle to be performed on you from without, lifting you above your fears and doubts and self-centeredness. You help God from within by turning in outgoing love to others, and miraculously your fears and doubts and self-centeredness will vanish. The miracle starts within, not from without.

—E. Stanley Jones

The game isn't over till it's over.

—Yogi Berra

If there is any kindness I can show, or any good thing I can do to any fellow being, let me do it now, and not deter or neglect it, as I shall not pass this way again.

—William Penn

If my film makes one more person feel miserable, I feel I've done my job.

—Woody Allen

O O O O O

This person called up and said, "You've got to come and take this seminar. It will completely change your life in just one weekend." And I said, "Well, I don't want to completely change my life this weekend. I've got a lot of things to do on Monday."

—Rick Fields

I don't want to get to the end of my life and find that I lived just the length of it. I want to have lived the width of it as well.

—Diane Ackerman

Even a lie is a psychic fact.

—Carl Jung

Never tell a lie when you can bullshit your way through.

—Arthur Abdel Simpson
Eric Ambler's *Dirty Story*

A lie can travel halfway around the world while the truth is putting on its shoes.

—Mark Twain

One must use a brazen lie to convince people of a reality of a higher and deeper order.

—Jean Cocteau

A story should have a beginning, a middle, and an end . . . but not necessarily in that order.

—Jean Luc Goddard

The pearl is the oyster's autobiography.

—Federico Fellini

Truth exists; only falsehood has to be invented.

—George Braque

We do not remember days, we remember moments.

—Cesare Pavese

Reminiscences make one feel so deliciously aged and sad.

—George Bernard Shaw

Life is all memory, except for the one present moment that goes by so quick you hardly catch it going.

—Tennessee Williams

I gave in, and admitted that God was God.

—C.S. Lewis

Inside my empty bottle I was constructing a lighthouse while all the others were making ships.

—Charles Simic

A story must be told in such a way that it constitutes help in itself. My grandfather was lame. Once they asked him to tell a story about his teacher. And he related how his teacher used to hop and dance while he prayed. My grandfather rose as he spoke, and he was so swept away by his story that he began to hop and dance to show how the master had done. From that hour he was cured of his lameness. That's how to tell a story.

—Martin Buber

○ ○ ○ ○ ○

Just throw away all that computerized shit listing all human data. No one knows anything about human beings. You have to love the people because they always lose.

—Leslie Woolf Hedley

I never realized how mediocre the world was until I got involved with some of its supposedly top people.

—Mason Williams

The gulf between knowledge and truth is infinite.

—Henry Miller

I have met on the street a very poor man who was in love. His hat was old, his coat was out at the elbows, the water passed through his shoes, and the stars through his soul.

—Victor Hugo

A low self-love in the parent desires that his child should repeat his character and fortune. I suffer whenever I see that common sight of a parent or senior imposing his opinion and way of thinking and being on a young soul to which he is totally unfit. Cannot we let people be themselves, and enjoy life in their own way? You are trying to make another you. One's enough.

—Ralph Waldo Emerson

Joy is not in things; it is in us.

—Richard Wagner

Nothing will change the fact that I cannot produce the least thing without absolute solitude.

—Johann Wolfgang von Goethe

Creation was given to men as a clean window through which the light of God could shine into men's souls. Sun and moon, night and day, rain, sea, the crops, the flowering tree, all these things were transparent. They spoke to man not of themselves but only of Him who made them. Nature was symbolic. But the progressive degradation of man after the fall led the Gentiles further and further from this truth. Nature became opaque.

—Thomas Merton

As for conforming outwardly, and living your own life inwardly, I do not think much of that.

—Henry David Thoreau

Moral indignation is jealousy with a halo.

—H.G. Wells

One stands perplexed and wonders whether one should use force or humble love. Always decide to use humble love! If you resolve on that once and for all, you may subdue the whole world.

—Fyodor Dostoyevsky

○ ○ ○ ○ ○

The void is the creatrix, the matrix. It is not mere hollowness and anarchy. But in women it has been identified with lovelessness, barrenness, sterility. We have been urged to fill our "emptiness" with children. We are not supposed to go down into the darkness of the core.

—Adrienne Rich

We are led one thing at a time to that pure gain—all that we lose.

—William Stafford

You can only hope to find a lasting solution to a conflict if you have learned to see the other objectively, but, at the same time, to experience their difficulties subjectively.

—Dag Hammarskjöld
Markings

Each of us must make our own true way, and when we do, that way will express the universal way.

—Suzuki Roshi

It is not healthy to be thinking all the time. Thinking is intended for acquiring knowledge or applying it. It is not essential living.

—Ernest Wood

We spend most of our time and energy in a kind of horizontal thinking. We move along the surface of things going from one quick base to another, often with a frenzy that wears us out.

We collect data, things, people, ideas, "profound experiences," never penetrating any of them. . . . But there are other times. There are times when we stop. We sit still. We lose ourselves in a pile of leaves or its memory. We listen and breezes from a whole other world begin to whisper. Then we begin our "going down."

—James Carroll

And so, for the first time in my life perhaps, I took the lamp and, leaving the zone of everyday occupations and relationships where everything seems clear, I went down into my inmost self, to the deepest abyss whence I feel dimly that my power of action emanates. But as I moved further and further away from the conventional certainties by which social life is superficially illuminated, I became aware that I was losing contact with myself. At each step of the descent a new person was disclosed within me of whose name I was no longer sure, and who no longer obeyed me. And when I had to stop my exploration because the path faded from beneath my steps, I found a bottomless abyss at my feet, and out of it comes—arising I know not from where—the current which I dare to call MY life.

—Teilhard de Chardin

New images of man do not spring from Policy Research reports. All cultures begin in explosions of myth in the minds of prophets, mystics, visionary scientists, artists, and crazies.

—William Irwin Thompson

The imagination is far better at inventing tortures than life because the imagination is a demon within us and it knows where to strike, where it hurts. It knows the vulnerable spot, and life does not, our friends and lovers do not, because seldom do they have the imagination equal to the task.

—Anaïs Nin

No one imagines that a symphony is supposed to improve in quality as it goes along, or that the whole object of playing it is to reach the finale. The point of music is discovered in every moment of playing and listening to it. It is the same, I feel, with the greater part of our lives, and if we are unduly absorbed in improving them we may forget altogether to live them.

—Alan Watts

I often think the Christian church suffers from a too ardent monotheism. In my house are many gods. With the boy, Jack Frost is ahead of Jesus, although we have never promoted Jack very hard. I see no harm in Jack and am not sure but what he ought to be taken into the church. He is a gifted spirit with an exciting technique and a rather gay program. And he is not terrible, like the Lord.

—E.B. White

○ ○ ○ ○ ○

In Holy Communion we have Christ under the appearance of bread. In our work we find him under the appearance of flesh and blood. It is the same Christ.

—Mother Theresa

Who never ate his bread with tears,
Who never sat weeping on his bed
During care-ridden nights
Knows you not, you heavenly powers.

—*Johann Wolfgang von Goethe*

The mystical union on the one hand. The resurrection of the body, on the other. I can't reach the ghost of an image, a formula, or even a feeling that combines them. But the reality we are given to understand, does. Reality the iconoclast once more. Heaven will solve our problems, but not, I think, by showing us the subtle reconciliations between all our apparently contradictory notions. The notions will all be knocked from under our feet. We shall see that there never was any problem.

—*C.S. Lewis*
A Grief Observed

. . . Time has two aspects. There is the arrow, the running river, without which there is no change, no progress, or direction, or creation. And there is the circle or the cycle, without which there is chaos, meaningless succession of instants, a world without clocks or seasons or promises.

—*Ursula K. LeGuin*
The Dispossessed

The Zen student, the poet, the husband, the wife—none knows with certainty what he or she is staying for, but all know the likelihood that they will be staying for "a while": to find out what they are staying for. And it is the faith of all those disciplines that they will not stay to find out that they should not have stayed.

—*Wendell Berry*

I am not bound by this vast work of creation. I am and I watch the drama of events.

—*Bhagavad Gita*

I have made a great discovery. I no longer believe in anything. . . . It is not the object that matters to me but what is between them: it is this "in-between" that is the real subject of my pictures. When one reaches this state of harmony between things and one's self, one reaches . . . a state of perfect freedom and peace—which makes everything possible and right. Life then becomes perpetual revelation.

—*George Braque*

True universality does not consist in knowing much but in loving much.

—*Jakob Burckhardt*

It seems as though I had not drunk from the cup of wisdom, but had fallen into it.

—*Sören Kierkegaard*

The only certainties that don't break down are those acquired in prayer.

—*Reinhold Schneider*

Being happy is a virtue too.

—*Ludwig Borne*

O O O O O

Disappointment is a good sign of basic intelligence. It cannot be compared to anything else: it is so sharp, precise, obvious, and direct. If we can open, then we suddenly begin to see that our expectations are irrelevant compared with the reality of the situations we are facing.

—Chogyam Trungpa

Exactitude in some small matters is the very soul of discipline.

—Joseph Conrad

Life, like a dome of many-colored glass, stains the white radiance of eternity.

—Percy Bysshe Shelley

Giving
Your life has brought you closer to your friends.
Yes, it has brought you home. All's well that ends.

—Robert Lowell

The sword embedded in the stone . . . it's a beautiful symbol, no one can get it out. Then someone comes along and takes it out with no effort because it was his sword. You have a woman who's made of stone. No one can remove his phallus from her. You come and remove it with no effort. You can do it because she is your woman. Because when she had the phallus inside her, it was immobile. Because it was yours. And you went through life castrated. But when you laid your pelvis against hers, you recovered your phallus and you were able to enter and withdraw with ease. And then water came from the stone. And that water fell on your testicles, and your testicles bloomed, like flowers.

—Alexandro Jodorowsky

You are a wish
to be here wishing yourself.

—Philip Whalen

When bad things happen, that's good. When good things happen, you don't need a philosophy.

—Mike Mathers

The strangest and most fantastic fact about negative emotions is that people actually worship them.

—P.D. Ouspensky

. . . You are no longer a Buddhist or a Hindu or a Christian or a Jew or a Moslem. You are love, you are truth. And love and truth have no form. They flow into forms. But the word is never the same as that which the word connotes. The word "God" is not God, the word "Mother" is not Mother, the word "Self" is not Self, the word "moment" is not the moment. All of these words are empty. We're playing at the level of intellect, feeding that thing in us that keeps wanting to understand. And here we are, all the words we've said are gone. Where did they go? Do you remember them all? Empty, empty. If you heard them, you are at this moment empty. You're ready for the next word. And the word will go through you. You don't have to know anything: that's what's so funny about it. You get so simple. You're empty. You know nothing. You simply are wisdom—not becoming anything, just being everything.

—Ram Dass

The key to the treasure is the treasure itself.

—John Barth

It doesn't matter who my father was; it matters who I remember he was.

—Anne Sexton

The mistake we make is to turn upon our past with angry wholesale negation. . . . The way of wisdom is to treat it airily, lightly, wantonly, and in a spirit of poetry; and above all to use its symbols, which are its spiritual essence, giving them a new connotation, a fresh meaning.

—John Cowper Powys

One day he was repairing the light fixture in the bathroom. He asked me to hold one of his hands and to grip the faucet of the bathtub with my other hand. I did this. Then he licked the index finger of his free hand and stuck it up into the empty socket where the lightbulb had been. As the electricity passed through him and into me and through me and was grounded in the faucet of the bathtub, my father kept saying, "Pal, I won't hurt you. I won't hurt you." If I had let go of the faucet, both of us would have died. If I had let go of his hand, he would have died.

—James Alan McPherson

Nobody writes if he or she has had a happy childhood.

—Joseph Hergesheimer

Oh beauty, why are you not enough?
Why am I crying after love?

—Sara Teasdale

How will the world end? The world will end in joy, because it is a place of sorrow. When joy has come, the purpose of the world has gone.

The world will end in peace, because it is a place of war. When peace has come, what is the purpose of the world? The world will end in laughter, because it is a place of tears. Where there is laughter, who can longer weep? In blessing it departs; it will not end as it began.

—A Course In Miracles

At the day of judgement, we shall not be asked what we have read but what we have done.

—Thomas à Kempis

Like every beginner, I thought you could beat, pummel, and thrash an idea into existence. Under such treatment, of course, any decent idea folds up its paws, turns on its back, fixes its eyes on eternity, and dies.

—Ray Bradbury

He liked to go from A to B without inventing letters between.

—John McPhee

O O O O O

One's own self is well hidden from one's own self: of all mines of treasure, one's own is the last to be dug up.

—Friedrich Nietzsche

When I don't write, I feel my world shrinking. I feel I am in a prison. I feel I lose my fire and my color. It should be a necessity, as the sea needs to heave, and I call it breathing.

—Anaïs Nin

Everywhere I go, I find a poet has been there before me.

—Sigmund Freud

For according to the outward man, we are in this world, and according to the inward man, we are in the inward world. . . . Since then we are generated out of both worlds, we speak in two languages, and we must be understood also by two languages.

—Jacob Boehme

Nothing can be attained without suffering but at the same time one must begin by sacrificing suffering.

—G.I. Gurdjieff

He begins to realize that the world was never outside himself, that it was his own dualistic attitude, the separation of "I" and "other" that created the problem. He begins to understand that he himself is making the walls solid, that he is imprisoning himself through his ambition. And so he begins to realize that to be free of his prison he must give up his ambition to escape and accept the walls as they are. . . . The more we try to struggle, the more we will discover that walls really are solid. The more energy we put into struggle, by that much will we strengthen the walls, because the walls need our attention to solidify them.

—Chögyam Trungpa
Cutting Through Spiritual Materialism

Man, man, I'm just scared of living. It's killing me.

—Mickey Spillane
The Deep

. . . It is impossible to define the meaning of life in a general way. Questions about the meaning of life can never be answered by sweeping statements. "Life" does not mean something vague, but something very real and concrete, just as life's tasks are also very real and concrete. They form man's destiny, which is different and unique for each individual. . . . When a man finds that it is his destiny to suffer, he will have to accept his suffering as his task, his single and unique task. . . . No one can relieve him of his suffering or suffer in his place. His unique opportunity lies in the way in which he bears his burden.

For us, as prisoners, these thoughts were not speculations far removed from reality. They were the only thoughts that could be of help to us. They kept us from despair, even when there was no chance of coming out of it alive.

—Viktor Frankl
Man's Search For Meaning

We have reason to be afraid. This is a terrible place.

—John Berryman

Compassion simply stated is leaving other people alone. You don't lay trips. You exist as a statement of your own level of evolution. You are available to another human being, to provide what they need, to the extent that they ask. But you begin to see that it is a fallacy to think that you can impose a trip on another person.

—Ram Dass

I do not take drugs—I am drugs.

—Salvador Dali

Mass seems to be over. Could hear them all at it. Pray for us. And pray for us. And pray for us. Good idea the repetition. Same thing with ads. Buy from us. And buy from us.

—James Joyce
Ulysses

○ ○ ○ ○ ○

More men die of their medicines than their diseases.

—Molière

No healing can take place until we decide to think actively about the dark side. Each of us has a dark side. If I shout at my small sons, I can say that I have a fatherly duty to discipline them, but we know that this shouting has a dark side. When so many whites moved to the suburbs in the Fifties, wasn't that a simple longing for open space? But it had a dark side. The dark side was that we let the centers of our cities disintegrate, in the same way that we let the

center of our psyche disintegrate. When entertainment, in the form of television, floods our house every night, we are only sitting and listening. This is a simple thing surely, isn't it? But it has a dark side. It has a very strong dark side, in that we don't have to entertain others, or enter any larger sort of community to be entertained.

—Robert Bly

Our difficulty is that human consciousness has not adjusted itself to a relational and integrated view of nature. We must see that consciousness is neither an isolated soul nor the mere function of a single nervous system, but of that totality of interrelated stars and galaxies which makes a nervous system possible.

—Alan Watts

How does one transcend himself; how does he open himself to new possibility? By realizing the truth of his situation, by dispelling the lie of his character, by breaking his spirit out of its conditioned prison. The enemy, for Kierkegaard as for Freud, is the Oedipus complex. The child has built up strategies and techniques for keeping his self-esteem in the face of the terror of his situation. These techniques become an armor that holds the person prisoner. The very defenses that he needs in order to move about with self-confidence and self-esteem become his lifelong trap. In order to transcend himself he must break down that which he needs in order to live. Like Lear he must throw off all his "cultural lendings" and stand naked in the storm of life. Kierkegaard had no illusions about man's urge to freedom. He knew how comfortable people were inside the prison of their character defenses. Like many prisoners they are comfortable in their limited and protected routines, and the idea of a parole into the wide world of chance, accident, and choice terrifies them.

—Ernest Becker
The Denial Of Death

What interests us is the uneasiness of Cezanne, the torments of van Gogh, that is to say the drama of the man. The rest is false.

—Pablo Picasso

What soap is for the body, tears are for the soul.

—Jewish proverb

Body and soul are not two substances but one. They are man becoming aware of himself in two different ways.

—C.F. von Weizsacker

We should all just smell well and enjoy ourselves more.

—Cary Grant

With ordinary consciousness you can't even begin to know what's happening.

—Saul Bellow
The Dean's December

○ ○ ○ ○ ○

We do not learn only from great minds; we learn from everyone, if only we observe and inquire. I received my greatest lesson in aesthetics from an old man in an Athenian *taverna*. Night after night he sat alone at the same table, drinking his wine with precisely the same movements. I finally asked him why he did this, and he said, "Young man, I first look at my glass to please my eyes, then I take it in my hand to please my hand, then I bring it to my nose to please my nostrils, and I am just about to bring it to my lips when I hear a small voice in my ears, 'How about me?' So I tap my glass on the table before I drink from it. I thus please all five senses."

—C.A. Doxiadis

Until one is committed, there is hesitancy, the chance to draw back, always ineffectiveness. . . . The moment one definitely commits oneself, then Providence moves, too. All sorts of things occur to help one that would never otherwise have occurred. . . . Boldness has genius, power, and magic in it. Begin it now.

—Johann Wolfgang von Goethe

All his earthly past will have been heaven to those who are saved. . . . The good man's past begins to change so that his forgiven sins and remembered sorrows take on the quality of heaven. . . . At the end of all things, the blessed will say, "We never lived anywhere but in heaven."

—C.S. Lewis

There is hunger for ordinary bread, and there is hunger for love, for kindness, for thoughtfulness; and this is the great poverty that makes people suffer so much.

—Mother Theresa

The kingdom of God is within you.

—Jesus

There can be no Kingdom of God in the world without the Kingdom of God in our hearts.

—Albert Schweitzer

In the coming world they will not ask me, "Why were you not Moses?" They will ask me, "Why were you not Zusya?"

—Zusya

There is no coming to heaven with dry eyes.

—Thomas Fuller

He who would be friends with God must remain alone or make the whole world his friend.

—Mahatma Gandhi

Be assured that if you knew all, you would pardon all.

—Thomas à Kempis

My obligation is this:
To be transparent.

—Pablo Neruda

You have to be completely without mercy on yourself. You can't say something like, "I did this yesterday before I played the concert and the concert was great! Therefore, I should do that again." Anything that creates a pattern creates an anchor. First it's conscious and then it's unconscious. When it's unconscious, it isn't only an anchor, it's a habit. . . . It's something everyone does at times. But for me the difference is—no matter what the beneficial effect of the thing—I cannot allow it to take the place of the dance. So it's the only way that the music is going to keep coming out. The music is dancing more than I am. I have to keep up with it by not having an anchor, so the music can take me somewhere.

—Keith Jarrett

The Delphic Oracle said that I was the wisest of all the Greeks. It is because I alone of all the Greeks know that I know nothing.

—Socrates

We have forgotten the age-old fact that God speaks chiefly through dreams and visions.

—Carl Jung

I reproach all modern religions for having handed to their believers consolations and glossings over of death, instead of administering to them the means of reconciling themselves to it and coming to an understanding with it. With it, with its full, unmasked cruelty: this cruelty is so tremendous that it is just with *it* that the circle closes: it leads right back again into the extreme of a mildness that is great, pure, and perfectly clear (all consolation is turbid) as we have never surmised mildness to be, not even on the sweetest spring day. But toward the experiencing of this most profound mildness which, were only a few of us to feel it with conviction, could perhaps little by little penetrate and make *transparent* all the relations of life: toward the experiencing of *this* richest and soundest mildness, mankind has never even taken the first steps—unless in its oldest, most innocent times, whose secret has been all but lost to us. The content of "initiations" was, I am sure, nothing but the imparting of a "key" that permitted the reading of the word "death" *without* negation; like the moon, life surely has a side permanently turned away from us which is not its counterpart but its complement towards perfection, toward consummation, toward the really sound and full sphere and orb of being.

—Rainer Maria Rilke

Understanding is the ultimate seduction of the mind. Go to the truth beyond the mind. Love is the bridge.

—Stephen Levine

It was the best of times, it was the worst of times; it was the age of wisdom, it was the age of foolishness; it was the epoch of belief, it was the epoch of incredulity; it was the season of light, it was the season of darkness; it was the spring of hope, it was the winter of despair.

—Charles Dickens

Most of the time I don't have much fun. The rest of the time I don't have any fun at all.

—Woody Allen

Every child is an artist. The problem is how to remain an artist once she grows up.

—Pablo Picasso

Nothing you write, if you hope to be good, will ever come out as you first hoped.

—Lillian Hellman

Who has fully realized that history is not contained in thick books but lives in our very blood?

—Carl Jung

The only thing that makes life possible is permanent, intolerable uncertainty: not knowing what comes next.

—Ursula K. LeGuin

Along with any broadening positive growth comes a broadening realization that we all stand on cracking ice.

—St. Luenza

To the extent that we honor all aspects of ourselves, we remove revulsion, self-hate, horror, and terror from our lives. As whole human beings we are the creatures of the greatest complexity on this planet. Respect for this complexity includes our insisting on acceptance of the inconsistent and incongruous.

—Theodore Rubin

The mind of man is capable of anything, because everything is in it, all the past as well as all the future.

—Joseph Conrad

My sacred world was autistic; that is to say, I had no wish to share it with others, nor could I have done so.

—W.H. Auden

Men are not free when they are doing just what they like. . . . Men are only free when they are doing what the *deepest self* likes. And there is getting down to the deepest self! It takes some diving.

—D.H. Lawrence

What is meant by light? To gaze with undimmed eyes on all darkness.

—Nikos Kazantzakis

The land is a mother that never dies.

—Maori saying

Light rare, untellable, lighting the very light. . . .

—Walt Whitman

No appointment, no disappointment.

—Swami Satchidananda

A machine is as distinctively and brilliantly and expressively human as a violin sonata or a theorem in Euclid.

—Gregory Vlastos

Narcissism: when one grows too old to believe in one's uniqueness, one falls in love with one's complexity.

—John Fowles

Fill the seats of justice with good men, not so absolute in goodness as to forget what human frailty is.

—Sir Thomas Noon Talfourd

In infatuation, the person is a *passive victim* of the spell of conceived attraction for the object. In love there is an *active appreciation* of the intrinsic worth of the object of love.

—Meher Baba

Crusaders for virtue are an awkward embarrassment to any society; they force us to make choices: either side with them, which is difficult and dangerous, or condemn them, which leads to self-betrayal.

—Edward Abbey

Success can eliminate as many options as failure.

—Tom Robbins
Even Cowgirls Get The Blues

No man should advocate a course in private that he's ashamed to admit in public.

—George McGovern

Perhaps everything terrible is in its deepest being something helpless that wants help from us.

—Rainer Maria Rilke
Letters To A Young Poet

○ ○ ○ ○ ○

"The Light," came the hoarse whisper, "the Clear Light. It's here—along with the pain, in spite of the pain."

"And where are you?"

"Over there, in the corner. I can see myself there. And she can see my body on the bed."

"Brighter," came the barely audible whisper, "brighter." And a smile of happiness intense almost to the point of elation transfigured her face.

Through his tears Dr. Robert smiled back at her. "So now you can let go, my darling." He stroked her gray hair. "Now you can let go. Let go," he insisted. "Let go of this poor old body. You don't need it anymore. Let it fall away from you. Leave it lying there like a pile of worn-out clothes. . . . Go on, go on into the Light, into the peace, into the living peace of the Clear Light."

—Aldous Huxley
Island

Once, in the Orient, I talked of suicide with a sage whose clear and gentle eyes seemed forever to be gazing at a never-ending sunset. "Dying is no solution," he affirmed. "And living?" I asked. "Nor living either," he conceded. "But, who tells you there is a solution?"

—Elie Wiesel

For what is it to die but to stand naked in the wind and to melt into the sun.

—Kahlil Gibran

To the question "Where does the soul go, when the body dies?" Jacob Boehme answered, "There is no necessity for it to go anywhere."

—Aldous Huxley
The Perennial Philosophy

The ideas that you have involving the nature of reality will strongly color your [after-death] experiences, for you will interpret them in the light of your beliefs, even as you now interpret daily life according to your ideas of what is possible or not possible. . . . A belief in hellfires can cause you to hallucinate Hades' conditions. A belief in a stereotyped heaven can result in a hallucination of heavenly conditions. You always form your own reality according to your ideas and expectations. This is the nature of consciousness in whatever reality it finds itself. Such hallucinations, I assure you, are temporary.

—Seth
Jane Roberts' *Seth Speaks*

To suffer one's death and to be reborn is not easy.

—Fritz Perls

Once Maharajji and Mr. Tewari were talking on the parapet at Hanuman Garh. Maharajji looked up above him and closed his eyes for a moment and told Tewari that a certain old woman devotee from down in the plains had just died. Then he giggled and laughed and laughed. Tewari, who had known Maharajji for many years, was taken aback and said, "You butcher! How can you laugh at the death of a human being?" Maharajji looked at him in surprise and said, "Would you rather have me pretend I'm one of the puppets?"

—Ram Dass
Miracle Of Love/Stories About Neem Karoli Baba

Why is it we are frightened of death?—as most people are. Frightened of what? Do please observe your own fears of what we call death—being frightened of coming to the end of the battle we call living. We are frightened of the unknown, what might happen; we are frightened of leaving the known things, the family, the books, the attachment to our house and furniture, to the people near us. We are frightened to let go of the things known; and the known is this living in sorrow, pain, and despair, with occasional flashes of joy; there is no end to this constant struggle; that is what we call living—of that we are frightened to let go. . . . Can

33

one die to everything that is "known," psychologically, from day to day? Can one die, psychologically, to all one's past, to all the attachments, fears, to the anxiety, vanity, and pride, so completely that tomorrow you wake up a fresh human being?

—J. Krishnamurti
The Flight Of The Eagle

Melnick says the soul is immortal and lives on after the body drops away, but if my soul exists without my body, I am convinced all my clothes will be loosefitting.

—Woody Allen
Without Feathers

If we live, we live; if we die, we die; if we suffer, we suffer; if we are terrified, we are terrified. There is no problem about it.

—Alan Watts
Beat Zen, Square Zen And Zen

Nature, immune as to a sacrifice of straw dogs,
Faces the decay of its fruits.
A sound man, immune as to a sacrifice of straw dogs,
Faces the passing of human generations.
The universe, like a bellows,
Is always emptying, always full:
The more it yields, the more it holds.

—Lao-tzu
The Way Of Life

In the Eastern tradition, the state of your consciousness at the last moment of life is so crucial that you spend your whole life preparing for that moment. We've had many assassinations in our culture recently and when we think what it was like for Bobby Kennedy or Jack Kennedy, if they had any thought, what it would have been. "Oh, I've been shot!" or "He did it," or "Goodbye," or "Get him," or "Forgive him." Mahatma Gandhi walked out into a garden to give a press conference and a gunman shot him three or four times, but as he was falling the only thing that came out of his mouth was, "Ram. . . ." The name of God. He was ready!

At the moment of death you let go lightly, you go out into the light, toward the One, toward God. The only thing that died, after all, was another set of thoughts of who you were this time around.

—Ram Dass
Grist For The Mill

"Only if one loves this earth with unbending passion can one relieve one's sadness," don Juan said. "A warrior is always joyful because his love is unalterable and his beloved, the earth, embraces him and bestows upon him inconceivable gifts. The sadness belongs only to those who hate the very thing that gives shelter to their beings."

Don Juan again caressed the ground with tenderness. "This lovely being, which is alive to its last recesses and understands every feeling, soothed me, it cured me of my pains, and finally when I had fully understood my love for it, it taught me freedom."

He paused. The silence around us was frightening. The wind hissed softly and then I heard the distant barking of a lone dog. . . .

"That dog's barking is the nocturnal voice of a man," don Juan said. "It comes from a house in that valley towards the south. A man is shouting through his dog, since they are companion slaves for life, his sadness, his boredom. He's begging his death to come and release him from the dull and dreary chains of life. . . . That barking, and the loneliness it creates, speaks of the feelings of men. Men for whom an entire life was like one Sunday afternoon, an afternoon which was not altogether miserable, but rather hot and dull and uncomfortable. They sweated and fussed a great deal. They didn't know where to go, or what to do. That afternoon left them only with the memory of petty annoyances and tedium, and then suddenly it was over; it was already night. . . . The antidote that kills that poison is here. . . . Only the love for this splendorous being can give freedom to a warrior's spirit; and freedom is joy, efficiency, and abandon in the face of any odds. That is the last lesson. It is always left for the last moment, for the moment of ultimate solitude when a man faces his death and his aloneness. Only then does it make sense."

—Carlos Castaneda
Tales Of Power

O O O O O

You don't tell the quality of a master by the size of his crowds.

—Richard Bach
Illusions

And the trouble is, if you don't risk anything, you risk even *more*.

—Erica Jong

The temptation to moralize is strong; it is emotionally satisfying to have enemies rather than problems, to seek out culprits rather than flaws in the system. God knows it is emotionally satisfying to be righteous with that righteousness that nourishes itself on the blood of sinners. But God also knows that what is emotionally satisfying can be spiritually devastating.

—William Sloane Coffin
The Courage To Love

"Yes," he said, "the cross is a good symbol to describe those two aspects of time. The vertical bar of the cross represents the eternal aspect of time, and the horizontal bar the aspect of passing time. Where the two bars cross, it is possible to see both times at once; the flashes of deep understanding that we have come from that point. But there is something else to consider. When we do not first accept things as they are, we are almost bound to want to change them by imposing our concept on perfection. We are working for our own selfish desires, from our egos. In a sense, we create another sort of time, imposed on that which is already perfect in essence."

—Reshad Feild
The Invisible Way

I guess I'm just an old mad scientist at bottom. Give me an underground laboratory, half a dozen atom-smashers, and a beautiful girl in a diaphanous veil waiting to be turned into a chimpanzee, and I care not who writes the nation's laws.

—S.J. Perelman

Those who hate you don't win unless you hate them back; and then you destroy yourself.

—Richard M. Nixon

One is not born a woman, one becomes one.

—Simone de Beauvoir

To the extent that most of us are users and consumers of energy and of a certain style of life, we are covertly giving the go-ahead to our government to protect those things for us. We must realize that inherent in every time you turn on the ignition of your car or climb into a jet plane, you are in some way part of a chain of reinforcing six percent of the world that's using about fifty percent of the natural resources. And that's not fair. We can't play "King of the Mountain" much longer. We're not respected by any of the poor people of the world at this point, because our humanitarian concerns have been overridden by our fear of loss of our "King of the Mountain" status.

—Ram Dass

If it happens that you are well off, in your heart be tranquil about it—if you can be just as glad and willing for the opposite condition. So let it be with food, friends, kindred, or anything else that God gives or takes away.

—Meister Eckhart

I am part of the sun as my eye is part of me. That I am part of the earth my feet know perfectly, and my blood is part of the sea. There is not any of me that is alone and absolute except my mind, and we shall find that the mind has no existence by itself, it is only the glitter of the sun on the surfaces of the water.

—D.H. Lawrence

Do you see a man who is wise in his own eyes? There is more hope for a fool than for him.

—*Proverbs* 26:12

A sight of happiness is happiness.

—Thomas Traherne

I never found the companion that was so companionable as solitude. We are for the most part more lonely when we go abroad among men than when we stay in our chambers. A man thinking or working is always alone, let him be where he will.

—Henry David Thoreau
Walden

Nature is visible thought.

—Heinrich Heine

If love is the answer, could you please rephrase the question?

—Lily Tomlin

○ ○ ○ ○ ○

A man's suffering is similar to the behavior of gas. If a certain quantity of gas is pumped into an empty chamber, it will fill the chamber completely and evenly, no matter how big the chamber. Thus suffering completely fills the human soul and conscious mind, no matter whether the suffering is great or little. Therefore, the "size" of human suffering is absolutely relative.

—Viktor Frankl
Man's Search For Meaning

Seeing Him alone, one transcends death; there is no other way.

—*The Upanishads*

Science is the art of creating suitable illusions which the fool believes or argues against, but the wise man enjoys for their beauty or their ingenuity, without being blind to the fact that they are human veils and curtains concealing the abysmal darkness of the unknowable.

—Carl Jung

Why is life so tragic; so like a little strip of pavement over an abyss? I look down; I feel giddy; I wonder how I am ever to walk to the end.

—Virginia Woolf

How different each death is, and yet it leads us into the self-same country, that country which we inhabit so rarely, where we see the worthlessness of what we have long pursued and will so soon return to pursuing.

—Iris Murdoch

Know that joy is rarer, more difficult, and more beautiful than sadness. Once you make this all-important discovery, you must embrace joy as a moral obligation.

—André Gide
Fruits Of The Earth

To do nothing is sometimes a good remedy.

—Hippocrates

The witch doctor succeeds for the same reason all the rest of us succeed. Each patient carries his own doctor inside him. They come to us not knowing that truth. We are at our best when we give the doctor who resides within each patient a chance to go to work.

—Albert Schweitzer

Life as we find it is too hard for us; it entails too much pain, too many disappointments, impossible tasks. We cannot do without palliative remedies. There are perhaps three of these means: powerful diversions of interest, which lead us to care little about our misery; substitutive gratifications, which lessen it; and intoxicating substances, which make us insensitive to it. Something of this kind is indispensible.

—Sigmund Freud

History is so indifferently rich that a case for almost any conclusion from it can be made by a selection of instances.

—Will Durant

At the moment you are prophesying in the desert, the fine pollen of an oak is falling to the ground and, in a century, will grow up into a forest.

—Jean Paul Richter

Life must be lived forwards, but can only be understood backwards.

—Sören Kierkegaard

The Indians long ago knew that music was going on permanently and that hearing it was like looking out a window at a landscape which didn't stop when one turned away.

—John Cage

It is invisible, and no hand can lay hold of it;
Intangible, and yet it can be felt
    everywhere. . . .
What is it? O wonder! What is it not? For it
    has no name.
In my foolishness, I tried to grasp it,
And I closed my hand, thinking that I held
    it fast:
But it escaped, and I could not retain it in my
    fingers.
Full of sadness, I unclenched my grip
And I saw it once again in the palm of my hand.
O unutterable wonder! O strange mystery!
Why do we trouble ourselves in vain? Why do
    we all wander astray!

—St. Symeon
The New Theologian

The man who writes about himself and his own time is the only man who writes about all people and about all time.

—George Bernard Shaw

I am writing the memoirs of a man who has lost his memory.

—Eugene Ionesco

Another way of approaching the thing is to consider it unnamed, unnameable.

—Frances Ponge

They always ask me if I'm happy when I'm finished with my work. Happy? Who's happy? What's happy? It's a dumb question.

—Paul Simon

We ought not to let ourselves be satisfied with the God we thought of, for when the thought slips our mind, that God slips with it. What we want is rather the reality of God, exalted far above any thought or creature.

—Meister Eckhart

Systems die; instincts remain.

—Oliver Wendell Holmes, Jr.

History, Stephen said, is a nightmare from which I am trying to awake.

—James Joyce

Reality can destroy the dream; why shouldn't the dream destroy reality?

—George Moore

For history you need a camera with two lenses— the telephoto and the kind of close-up with a fine, penetrating focus. You can forget the wide-angle lens; there is no angle wide enough.

—John Irving

A man is infinitely more complicated than his thoughts.

—Paul Valéry

Won't you come into the garden? I would like my roses to see you.

—Richard B. Sheridan

○ ○ ○ ○ ○

All of life is the exercise of risk.

—William Sloan Coffin

Dwell as near as possible to the channel in which your life flows.

—Henry David Thoreau

As far as the Buddha nature is concerned, there is no difference between sinner and sage. . . . One enlightened thought and one is a Buddha, one foolish thought and one is an ordinary man.

—Hui Neng

God is my ground, I am God's ground.

—Meister Eckhart

Illusion. First there is the illusion of perfect accord, then revelation by experience of the many differences, and then I come upon a cross-road, and unless there is a definite betrayal, I finally accept the complete person.

—Anaïs Nin

The higher goal of spiritual living is not to amass a wealth of information, but to face sacred moments.

—Rabbi Abraham Heschel

Once upon a time a man whose ax was missing suspected his neighbor's son.

The boy walked like a thief, looked like a thief, and spoke like a thief.

But the man found his ax while digging in the valley, and the next time he saw his neighbor's son, the boy walked, looked, and spoke like any other child.

—Lao-tzu

There is a time for expanding and a time for contraction; one provokes the other and the other calls for the return of the first. . . . Never are we nearer the Light than when darkness is deepest.

—Swami Vivekananda

Let us not be satisfied with just giving money. Money is not enough, money can be got, but they need your hearts to love them. So, spread your love everywhere you go; first of all in your own home. Give love to your children, to your wife or husband, to a next-door neighbor.

—Mother Theresa

It is a serious thing to live in a society of possible gods and goddesses, to remember that the dullest and most uninteresting person you can talk to may one day be a creature which, if you saw it now, you would be strongly tempted to worship, or else a horror and corruption such as

you now meet, if at all, only in nightmare. All day long we are, in some degree, helping each other to one or the other of these destinations. It is in the light of these overwhelming possibilities, it is the awe and circumspection proper to them that we should conduct all our dealings with one another, all friendships, all loves, all play, all politics. There are no *ordinary* people. You have never talked to a mere mortal.

—C.S. Lewis
Screwtape Proposes A Toast, And Other Pieces

○ ○ ○ ○ ○

Ah, don't let my prayer seem too little to You, God. You sit up there, so white and old, with all the angels about You and the stars slipping by. And I come to You with a prayer about a telephone call. Ah, don't laugh, God. You see, You don't know how it feels. You're so safe, there on Your throne, with the blue swirling under You. Nothing can touch You; no one can twist Your heart in his hands. This is suffering, God, this is bad, bad suffering.

—Dorothy Parker
A Telephone Call

The physical senses actually can be said to create the physical world, in that they force you to perceive an available field of energy in physical terms, and impose a highly specialized pattern upon this field of reality. Using the physical senses, you can perceive reality in no other way.

—Seth
Jane Roberts' *Seth Speaks*

"There is nothing to fear." This simply states a fact. It is not a fact to those who believe in illusions, but illusions are not facts. In truth there is nothing to fear.

—*A Course In Miracles*

One day when the Sultan was in his palace at Damascus a beautiful youth who was his favorite rushed into his presence, crying out in great agitation that he must fly at once to Baghdad, and imploring leave to borrow his Majesty's swiftest horse.

The Sultan asked why he was in such haste to go to Baghdad.

"Because," the youth answered, "as I passed through the gardens of the palace just now, Death was standing there, and when he saw me he stretched out his arms as if to threaten me, and I must lose no time in escaping from him."

The young man was given leave to take the Sultan's horse and fly, and when he was gone the Sultan went down indignantly into the garden, and found Death still there. "How dare you make threatening gestures at my favorite?" he cried; but Death, astonished, answered, "I assure your Majesty I did not threaten him. I only threw up my arms in surprise at seeing him here, because I have a tryst with him tonight in Baghdad."

—Edith Wharton
A Backward Glance

Every moment and every event of every man's life plants something in his soul. For just as the wind carries thousands of winged seeds, so each

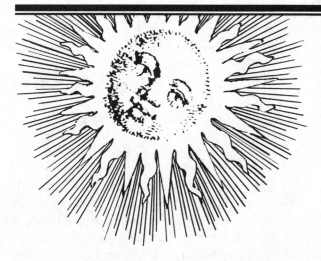

moment brings with it germs of spiritual vitality that come to rest imperceptibly in the minds and wills of men. Most of these unnumbered seeds perish and are lost, because men are not prepared to receive them. For such seeds as these cannot spring up anywhere, except in the good soil of freedom, spontaneity, and love.

—Thomas Merton

Good for the body is the work of the body, and good for the soul is the work of the soul, and good for either is the work of the other.

—Henry David Thoreau

A man can only do what he can do. But if he does that each day he can sleep at night and do it again the next day.

—Albert Schweitzer

○ ○ ○ ○ ○

If you have any notion of where you are going, you will never get anywhere.

—Joan Miró

I refuse to be intimidated by reality anymore. What is reality? Nothing but a collective hunch.

—Lily Tomlin

Dreams are real while they last; can we say more of life?

—Havelock Ellis

When our first parents were driven out of Paradise, Adam is believed to have remarked to Eve, "My dear, we live in an age of transition."

—Dean Inge

Have you ever sat very quietly without any movement? You try it, sit really still, with your back straight, and observe what your mind is doing. Don't try to control it, don't say it should not jump from one thought to another, but just be aware of how your mind is jumping. Don't do anything about it, but watch it as from the banks of a river you watch the river flow by. In the flowing river there are so many things—fishes, leaves, dead animals—but it is always living, moving, and your mind is like that. It is everlastingly restless, flitting from one thing to another like a butterfly . . . just watch your mind. It is great fun. If you try it as fun, as an amusing thing, you will find that the mind begins to settle down without any effort on your part to control it. There is then no censor, no judge, no evaluator; and when the mind is thus very quiet of itself, spontaneously still, you will discover what it is to be gay. Do you know what gaiety is? It is just to laugh, to take delight in anything or nothing, to know the joy of living, smiling, looking straight into the face of another without any sense of fear.

—J. Krishnamurti
Think On These Things

Make your ego porous. Will is of little importance, complaining is nothing, fame is nothing. Openness, patience, receptivity, solitude is everything.

—Rainer Maria Rilke

The human condition is such that pain and effort are not just symptoms which can be removed without changing life itself; they are rather the modes in which life itself, together with the necessity to which it is bound, makes itself felt. For mortals, the "easy life of the gods" would be a lifeless life.

—Hannah Arendt

We have to endure the discordance between imagination and fact. It is better to say, "I am suffering" than to say, "This landscape is ugly."

—Simone Weil

I'll play it first and tell you what it is later.

—Miles Davis

○ ○ ○ ○ ○

I do not much believe in education. Each man ought to be his own model, however frightful that may be.

—Albert Einstein

Education consists mainly in what we have unlearned.

—Mark Twain

To know how to suggest is the great art of teaching.

—Ralph Waldo Emerson

We must learn to get on in the world—not in the commercial and materialistic sense, but as a means of getting heavenward. Any education which neglects this fact, and to the extent to which it neglects it, is false education, because it is false to man.

—Eric Gill

I respect faith but doubt is what gets you an education.

—Wilson Mizner

So many things fail to interest us, simply because they don't find in us enough surfaces on which to live, and what we have to do is to increase the number of planes in our mind, so that a much larger number of themes can find a plane in it at the same time.

—José Ortega y Gasset

What you are looking for is who is looking.

—St. Francis of Assisi

If we had a keen vision of all ordinary life, it would be like hearing the grass grow or the squirrel's heart beat, and we should die of the roar which lies on the other side of silence. As it is, the quickest of us walk about well-wadded with stupidity.

—George Eliot

I am not worried about possessions anymore, but each one of them tells a story. I notice the objects, rugs, furniture, and photographs and am reminded of the lessons that needed to be learned at that time. I consciously remember, so that I don't forget again. It is an art—to recollect an experience in past time, knowing that in reality there is no such thing, and to bring the experience into present time is a useful form. The key is relatively simple, and that is that we are continuously being given experiences, out of which we can learn. Once understood, we do not need the experience anymore. Perhaps the greatest teacher and lesson of all is life itself.

—Reshad Feild
The Invisible Way

The truth knocks on the door and you say, "Go away, I'm looking for the truth," and so it goes away.

—Robert M. Pirsig
Zen And The Art Of Motorcycle Maintenance

I used to be Snow White, but then I drifted.

—Mae West

One day it was announced by Master Joshu that the young monk Kyogen had reached an enlightened state. Much impressed by this news, several of his peers went to speak with him.

"We have heard that you are enlightened. Is this true?" his fellow students inquired.

"It is," Kyogen answered.

"Tell us," said a friend, "how do you feel?"

"As miserable as ever," replied the enlightened Kyogen.

—Source unknown
quoted in Joe Hymas' *Zen In The Martial Arts*

There are no perfect beings, and there never will be.

—Henry Miller

While it's summer people say
Winter is the better season.
Such is human reason!

—Kamijima Onitsura

It's amazing how potent cheap music can be.

—Noel Coward

When a piece enters the soul of a man who knows music, autumn seems eternal from the terrace.

—Chen Hung-Shou

The magic of children is their ability to cloud our memories so that when we look back we recall only the golden moments, the sweet laughter and the sentimental tears, and none of the awful trials.

—Russell Baker

O O O O O

Each phenomenon on earth is an allegory, and each allegory is an open gate through which the soul, if it is ready, can pass into the interior of the world where you and I and day and night are all one. In the course of his life, every

43

human being comes upon that open gate, here or there along the way; everyone is sometimes assailed by the thought that everything visible is an allegory and that behind the allegory live spirit and eternal life. Few, to be sure, pass through the gate and give up the beautiful illusion for the surmised reality of what lies within.

—Hermann Hesse
Strange News From Another Star

Freedom is what you do with what's been done to you.

—Jean-Paul Sartre

Be regular and orderly in your life like a bourgeois, so that you may be violent and original in your work.

—Gustave Flaubert

The universe isn't run on the point system. And survival isn't what it's all about. Do what you're going to do; and with humor be aware that you might as well be doing the opposite.

—R.K. Welsh

Inside yourself or outside, you never have to change what you see, only the way you see it.

—Thaddeus Golas

It takes seven years to get over the stink of enlightenment.

—Source unknown

. . . The path without a heart will turn against men and destroy them. It does not take much to die, and to seek death and to seek nothing.

—Carlos Castaneda
The Teachings Of Don Juan

I don't fear death because I don't fear anything I don't understand. When I start to think about it, I order a massage and it goes away.

—Hedy Lamarr
Ecstasy And Me

The tragedy and the magnificence of Homo Sapiens together rise from the same smoky truth that we alone among the animal species refuse to acknowledge natural law.

—Robert Ardrey
The Social Contract

One must have apocalypse in one eye and the millennium in the other, and as you look out through that double vision, the third eye develops and sees the resolution of tragedy and conflict and the rest of it.

—William Irwin Thompson

The most incomprehensible thing about the world is that it is comprehensible.

—Albert Einstein

Take from others what you want, but never be a disciple of anyone.

—A.S. Neill

○ ○ ○ ○ ○

I took a deep breath and listened to the old brag of my heart. I am, I am, I am.

—Sylvia Plath

The universe is made of stories, not of atoms.

—Muriel Rukeyser

In my sex fantasy, nobody ever loves me for my mind.

—Nora Ephron

There are only two or three human stories, and they go on repeating themselves as fiercely as if they had never happened before.

—Willa Cather

Good habits are worth being fanatical about.

—John Irving
Setting Free The Bears

Courage is the price that Life exacts for granting peace.

—Amelia Earhart

Thus, those who say that they would have right without its correlate, wrong, or good government without its correlate, misrule, do not apprehend the great principles of the universe, nor the nature of all creation. One might as well talk of the existence of heaven without that of earth, or of the negative principle without the positive, which is clearly impossible. Yet people keep on discussing it without stop; such people must be either fools or knaves.

—Chuang Tzu

To punish and destroy the oppressor is merely to initiate a new cycle of violence and oppression. The only real liberation is that which liberates both the oppressor and the oppressed at the same time from the same tyrannical automatism of the violent process which contains in itself the curse of irreversibility.

—Thomas Merton
Gandhi On Non-Violence

I have come to the conclusion, after many years of sometimes sad experience, that you cannot come to any conclusion at all.

—Vita Sackville-West

I hate
this wretched willow soul of mine,
patiently enduring, plaited or twisted
by other hands.

—Karin Boye

Whoever wants to see a brick must look at its pores, and must keep his eyes close to it. But whoever wants to see a cathedral cannot see it as he sees a brick. This demands a respect for distance.

—José Ortega y Gasset

O O O O O

I have no money, no resources, no hopes. I am the happiest man alive.

—Henry Miller

Politicians wish to move great masses of people. We do not need to move great masses of anyone. We need to let the bitterness of the moves we have already accomplished die down.

—Stephen Gaskin

On a hot day in the southern desert of Africa I had wanted to go and speak to one of my favorite Stone Age hunters. He was sitting in the middle of a thorn bush. . . . He was huddled in an attitude of the most intense concentration . . . but his friends would not let me get near

him, saying, "But don't you know, he is doing work of the utmost importance. He is making clouds."

—Laurens Van der Post

The best people possess a feeling for beauty, the courage to take risks, the discipline to tell the truth, the capacity for sacrifice. Ironically, their virtues make them vulnerable; they are often wounded, sometimes destroyed.

—Ernest Hemingway
A Farewell To Arms

The Eskimos had fifty-two names for snow because it was important to them: there ought to be as many for love.

—Margaret Atwood

Arnold Bennett says that the horror of marriage lies in its "dailiness." All acuteness of relationship is rubbed away by this. The truth is more like this: life—say four days out of seven—becomes automatic; but on the fifth day a bead of sensation (between husband and wife) forms which is all the fuller and more sensitive because of the automatic customary unconscious days on either side. That is to say, the year is marked by moments of great intensity, Hardy's "moments of vision." How can a relationship endure for any length of time except under these conditions?

—Virginia Woolf

The main point of any spiritual practice is to step out of the bureaucracy of ego. This means stepping out of ego's constant desire for a higher, more spiritual, more transcendental version of knowledge, religion, virtue, judgement, comfort, or whatever it is that the particular ego is seeking. One must step out of spiritual materialism.

—Chögyam Trungpa
Cutting Through Spiritual Materialism

We are all killers.

—Albert Camus

As you grow older you will find that your desires are never really fulfilled. In fulfillment there is always the shadow of frustration, and in your heart there is not a song but a cry. The desire to become—to become a great man, a great saint, a great this or that—has no end and therefore no fulfillment; its demand is ever for the "more," and such desire always breeds agony, misery, wars. But when one is free of all desire to become, there is a state of being whose action is totally different. It is. That which is has no time. It does not think in terms of fulfillment. Its very being is in its fulfillment.

—J. Krishnamurti
Think On These Things

○ ○ ○ ○ ○

The soul should always stand ajar, ready to welcome the ecstatic experience.

—Emily Dickinson

Each of us must make his own true way, and when we do, that way we will express the universal way.

—Suzuki Roshi
Zen Mind, Beginner's Mind

If you are doing something you would do for nothing then you are on your way to salvation. And if you could drop it in a minute and forget the outcome, you are even further along. And if while you are doing it you are transported into another existence, there is no need for you to worry about the future.

—George A. Sheehan

. . . Consciously, or unconsciously, the human being seeks to find a material form for the new value which lives in him in spiritual form. That is the searching of the spiritual value for materialization. Matter is here a storeroom and from it the spirit chooses what is specifically necessary for it—just as the cook would. That is the positive, the creative. That is the good. The white, fertilizing ray. This white ray leads to evolution, to elevation. Thus behind matter the creative spirit is concealed within matter.

—Wassily Kandinsky

In the miraculous spontaneity of the sun, there is discipline that utterly escapes you, and a knowledge beyond any that we know. And in the spontaneous playing of the bees from flower to flower, there is a discipline beyond any that you know, and laws that follow their own knowledge and joy that is beyond command. For true discipline, you see, is found only in spontaneity.

—Seth
Jane Roberts' *Seth Speaks*

Let mystery have its place in you; do not be always turning up your whole ploughshare of self-examination, but leave a little fallow corner in your heart ready for any seed the wind may bring, and reserve a nook of shadow for the passing bird; keep a place in your heart for the unexpected guest, an altar for the unknown God.

—Henri Frédéric Amiel

If I speak with the eloquence of men and of angels, but have no love, I become no more than blaring brass or crashing cymbal. If I have the gift of foretelling the future and hold in my hand not only all human knowledge but the very secrets of God, and if I also have that absolute faith which can move mountains, but have no love, I amount to nothing at all. If I dispose of all that I possess, yes even if I give my own body to be burned, but have no love, I achieve precisely nothing.

This love of which I speak is slow to lose patience —it looks for a way of being constructive. It is not possessive; it is neither anxious to impress nor does it cherish inflated ideas of its own importance.

Love knows no limit to its endurance, no end to its trust, no fading of its hope; it can outlast anything. It is, in fact, the one thing that still stands when all else has fallen.

—St. Paul
1 Corinthians

He who would know the world, seek first within his being's depths; he who would truly know himself, develop interest in the world.

—Rudolf Steiner

○ ○ ○ ○ ○

Somehow the realization that nothing was to be hoped for had a salutary effect upon me. For weeks and months, for years, in fact, all my life I had been looking forward to something happening, some extrinsic event that would alter my life, and now suddenly, inspired by the absolute hopelessness of everything, I felt relieved, as if a great burden had been lifted from my shoulders.

—Henry Miller
Tropic Of Cancer

We do not understand that life is paradise, for it suffices only to wish to understand it, and at once paradise will appear in front of us in its beauty.

—Fyodor Dostoyevsky
The Brothers Karamazov

I exist as I am, that is enough,
If no other in the world be aware I sit content,
And if each and all be aware I sit content.

One world is aware and by far the largest to me,
    and that is myself,
And whether I come to my own today or in ten
    thousand or ten million years,
I can cheerfully take it now, or with equal cheer-
    fulness I can wait.

My foothold is tenon'd and mortis'd in granite,
I laugh at what you call dissolution,
And I know the amplitude of time.

—Walt Whitman
Song Of Myself

Mind invented contradictions, invented names; it called some things beautiful, some ugly, some

good, some bad. One part of life was called love, another murder. How young, foolish, comical this mind was. One of its inventions was time. A subtle invention, a refined instrument for torturing the self even more keenly and making the world multiplex and difficult. For then man was separated from all he craved only by time, by time alone, this crazy invention! It was one of the props, one of the crutches that you had to let go, that one above all, if you wanted to be free.

—Hermann Hesse
Klein And Wagner

Never try to teach a pig how to sing. It wastes your time and annoys the pig.

—Source unknown

You must begin to trust yourself sometime. I suggest you do it now. If you do not then you will forever be looking to others to prove your own merit to you, and you will never be satisfied. You will always be asking others what to do, and at the same time resenting those from whom you seek such aid. It will seem to you that their experience is legitimate and yours counterfeit. You will feel shortchanged. You will find yourself exaggerating the negative aspects of your life, and the positive sides of other people's experiences. You are a multidimensional personality. Trust the miracle of your own being. Make no divisions between the physical and the spiritual in your lifetime, for the spiritual speaks with a physical voice and the corporeal body is the creation of the spirit.

—Seth
Jane Roberts' *The Nature Of Personal Reality*

Life is far too important a thing ever to talk about.

—Oscar Wilde

It is better to give and receive.

—Bernard Gunther

Around the table of death and life, bread and wine, where we can still meet each other, there are sounds to hear if we listen carefully. There is the sound of going down into the abyss and being lifted up, heart and body, not to heaven but to the good earth. There are the sounds of the lively ghosts of God, laughing still with love. There are the sounds of men and women stirring, standing. There is the sound of the season's changing. And wine. There is the sound of the day breaking. And bread.

—James Carroll

You don't have to suffer continual chaos in order to grow.

—John C. Lilly

When you sit with a nice girl for two hours you think it's only a minute. But when you sit on a hot stove for a minute you think it's two hours. That's relativity.

—Albert Einstein

I am a mind and as mind I existed before fear and will continue after it has passed. I do not have to wrap my attention so tightly around some form of distress that I come to believe I have changed. Possibly all feelings of personal unworthiness stem from this confusion of two dissimilar things. Yet my freedom lies in the truth that what I am is still present and can be seen within a broader view. What is needed is the willingness to look around calmly and to let all interpretations be still.

—Hugh Prather
There Is A Place Where You Are Not Alone

Ramana Maharshi had cancer of the arm and he wouldn't have it treated and the devotees said, "Oh Bhagavan—God—take care of your body." And he said, "No, it has finished its work on this plane." They said, "Don't leave us; don't leave us." And he looked at them like he was bewildered, and he said, "Where can I go? Just because you're not going to see me on the plane you're addicted to, do you think I'm going anywhere?"

—Ram Dass
The Only Dance There Is

Once again I tried committing suicide—this time by wetting my nose and inserting it into the light socket. Unfortunately, there was a short in the wiring, and I merely caromed off the icebox. Still obsessed by thoughts of death, I brood constantly. I keep wondering if there is an afterlife, and if there is, will they be able to break a twenty?

—Woody Allen
Without Feathers

○ ○ ○ ○ ○

She say, My first step from the old white man was trees. Then air. Then birds. Then other people. But one day when I was sitting quiet and feeling like a motherless child, which I was, it came to me: that feeling of being part of everything, not separate at all. I knew that if I cut a tree, my arm would bleed. And I laughed and I cried and I run all around the house. I just knew what it was. In fact, when it happen, you can't miss it.

—Alice Walker
The Color Purple

If you begin to understand what you are without trying to change it, then what you are undergoes a transformation.

—J. Krishnamurti

What we commonly call man, the eating, drinking, planting, counting man, does not, as we know him, represent himself, but misrepresents himself. Him we do not respect, but the soul, whose organ he is, would he let it appear through his action, would make our knees bend. When it breathes through his intellect, it is genius; when it breathes through his will, it is virtue; when it flows through his affection, it is love.

—Ralph Waldo Emerson
The Over-Soul

Two things come to mind that are euphoric for me. One is the universal euphoric: sex, that period of time when you are at an absolute peak of sexual feeling. The other is when I create something that moves me. When I am the audience to my own creation and I'm moved. If it were a drug and I could buy it, I'd spend all my money on it.

—Paul Simon

Whatever the next thing is I write, it's got to be even more naked than the last.

—Harold Pinter

Everywhere in the world one has to pay for the right to live on one's own naked spiritual reserves.

—Boris Pasternak

Where the spirit does not work with the hand there is no art.

—Leonardo Da Vinci

I measure time
by how the body sways.

—Theodore Roethke

The function of dreams is to teach the waking mind how to forget what it thinks it knows but doesn't.

—William R. Stimson

There's a mystery dimension in myth—there always is, and you can't put a ring around it. It's the difference between drawing a circle on the ground and dropping a pebble into a pond from which circles go out. The myth drops a pebble into a pond, it tells you of a certain center, it puts you on a certain center—what the Navajo call the pollen path of beauty—but it doesn't give you a definition.

—Joseph Campbell

Through pride we are ever deceiving ourselves. But deep down below the surface of the average conscience a still, small voice says to us, "Something is out of tune."

—Carl Jung

Man is afraid of things that cannot harm him, and he knows it, and he craves things that cannot be of help to him, and he knows it; but in truth the one thing man is afraid of is within himself and the one thing he craves is within himself.

—*The Tales Of Rabbi Nachman*
translated by Martin Buber

○ ○ ○ ○ ○

We cannot live only for ourselves. A thousand fibers connect us with our fellow men; and among those fibers, as sympathetic threads, our actions run as causes, and they come back to us as effects.

—Herman Melville

I am certainly not radical enough. One can never be radical enough; that is, one must always be as radical as reality itself.

—Vladimir Ilyich Lenin

The role of the artist is tragic today because, while the world's horizons have been extended, the human heart is as small as ever.

—Marc Chagall

Is it progress if a cannibal uses a knife and fork?

—Stanislaw J. Lec

Each one of us, as long as life stirs in him, may play a part in extricating himself from the power system by asserting his primacy as a person in quiet acts of mental or physical withdrawal—in gestures of non-conformity, in abstentions, restrictions, inhibitions, which will liberate him from the domination of the pentagon of power.

—Lewis Mumford

A man who is willing to undertake the discipline and the difficulty of mending his own ways is worth more to the conservation movement than a hundred who are insisting merely that the government and industries mend *their* ways.

—Wendell Berry

There will be less external discipline the more internal discipline there is.

—Simone Weil

And I recall an account of Trollope going up to London to pick up a rejected manuscript from a publisher, getting on the train to return home, laying the bulky bundle on his lap face down, and beginning a new book on the back pages of the rejected one.

—Source unknown
Quoted in Richard Kehl's *Silver Departures*

Home is not where you live but where they understand you.

—Christian Morgenstern

I believe that every man and woman represents humanity. We are different as to intelligence,

health, talents. Yet we are all one. We are all saints and sinners, adults and children, and no one is anyone's superior or judge. We have all been awakened with the Buddha, crucified with Christ, and we have all killed and robbed with Genghis Khan, Stalin, and Hitler.

I believe that man can visualize the experience of the whole universal man only by realizing his individuality and never by trying to reduce himself to an abstract, common denominator. Man's task in life is the paradoxical one of realizing his individuality and at the same time transcending it to arrive at the experience of universality. Only the fully developed self can drop the ego.

—Erich Fromm

I do not ask of God that He should change anything in events themselves, but that He should change me in regard to things, so that I might have the power to create my own universe, to govern my dreams, instead of enduring them.

—Gérard de Nerval

You are here to aid in the great expansion of consciousness. You are not here to cry about the miseries of the human condition but to change them when you do not find them to your liking through the joy, strength, and vitality that is within you; to create the spirit as faithfully and beautifully as you can in flesh.

—Seth
Jane Roberts' *The Nature Of Personal Reality*

Sport is where an entire life can be compressed into a few hours, where the emotions of a lifetime can be felt on an acre or two of ground, where a person can suffer and die and rise again on six miles of trails through a New York City park. Sport is a theater where sinner can turn saint and a common man become an uncommon hero, where the past and future can fuse with the present. Sport is singularly able to give us peak experiences where we feel completely one with the world and transcend all conflicts as we finally become our own potential.

—George A. Sheehan

Men of sensitivity are like good, much-played violins which vibrate at each touch of the bow.

—Wassily Kandinsky

The most important tool the artist fashions through constant practice is faith in his ability to produce miracles when they are needed.

—Mark Rothko

It is disastrous to name ourselves.

—Willem de Kooning

The Lord possessed me in the beginning of His ways, before He made anything from the beginning. I was set up from eternity, and of old before the Earth was made. . . . I was with Him forming all things: and was delighted every day, playing before Him at all times; playing in the world. And my delights were to be with the children of men.

—*Proverbs 8:22–23*
30–31

Political solutions work as long as the situation is hopeless.

—J.R. Slaughter

The secret of improved plant breeding, apart from scientific knowledge, is love. While I was conducting experiments to make spineless cacti, I often talked to the plants. . . . "You have nothing to fear," I would tell them. "You don't need your defensive thorns. I will protect you." Gradually the useful plant of the desert emerged in a thornless variety.

—Luther Burbank
to Paramahansa Yogananda

Your body is the temple of your soul. Your soul is God's temple. You cannot get to your heavenly Father until you take care of your earthly mother, which is your body.

—Hari Dass

In order *to do* it is necessary *to be*. And it is necessary first to understand what *to be* means.

—P.D. Ouspensky
In Search Of The Miraculous

They are so concerned for their life that their anxiety makes life unbearable, even when they have the things they think they want. Their very concern for enjoyment makes them unhappy. . . .

I will hold to the saying that: "Perfect joy is to be without joy. Perfect praise is to be without praise."

If you ask "what ought to be done" and "what ought not to be done" on earth in order to produce happiness, I answer that these questions do not have an answer. There is no way of determining such things. . . .

—Thomas Merton
The Way Of Chuang Tzu

There is no need to struggle to be free; the absence of struggle is in itself freedom.

—Chögyam Trungpa
Cutting Through Spiritual Materialism

○ ○ ○ ○ ○

O Lord, give me chastity and continency, but not yet.

—St. Augustine

Poverty is not the absence of goods, but rather the overabundance of desire.

—Plato

Everything in nature is lyrical in its ideal essence, tragic in its fate, and comic in its existence. Being, then, is the dazzle each of us makes as we thread the dance of those three rhythms of our lives.

—George Santayana

"You understand," said Chaydem, "but the reality of it escapes you. Understanding is nothing. The eyes must be kept open, constantly. To open your eyes you must relax, not strain. Don't be afraid of falling backwards into a bottomless pit. There is nothing to fall into. You're in it and of it, and one day, if you persist, you will be it. I don't say you will have it, *please* notice, because there's nothing to possess. Neither are

you to be possessed, remember that! You are to liberate your self. There are no exercises, physical, spiritual, to practice. All such things are like incense—they awaken a feeling of holiness. We must be holy without holiness. We must be whole . . . complete. That's being holy. Any other kind of holiness is false, a snare, and a delusion. . . ."

—Henry Miller
Plexus

To laugh often and much; to win the respect of intelligent people and the affection of children; to earn the appreciation of honest criticism and endure the betrayal of false friends; to appreciate beauty and find the best in others; to leave the world a bit better whether by a healthy child, a garden patch, a redeemed social condition; to know even one life has breathed easier because you have lived—this is to have succeeded.

—Ralph Waldo Emerson

The manifesto of the person . . . marks one of the great turning points in the human story. . . . We may come to see that tribe, nation, class, social movement, revolutionary masses . . . that all these have, like shadows that eclipse the sun, gained their existence at the expense of something far brighter and more beautiful: our essential and still unexplored self. And, recognizing that truth, we may seek to replace these "higher" social allegiances with an astonishing ethical proposition—*that all people are created to be persons*, and that persons come first, before all collective fictions.

—Theodore Roszak
Person/Planet

This oceanic feeling of wonder is the common source of religious mysticism, of pure science and art for art's sake; it is their common denominator and emotional bond.

—Arthur Koestler
The Act Of Creation

Argue for your limitations, and sure enough, they're yours.

—Richard Bach

It's hard to face that open space.

—Neil Young

We want our minds to be clear—not so we can think clearly, but so we can be open in our perceptions.

—M.C. Richards

Do not confine your children to your own learning, for they were born in another time.

—Hebrew proverb

Being, not doing, is my first joy.

—Theodore Roethke

○ ○ ○ ○ ○

The art of medicine consists of amusing the patient while nature cures the disease.

—Voltaire

Man is made by his belief. As he believes, so he is.

—*Bhagavad Gita*

Your pain is the breaking of the shell that encloses your understanding.

—Kahlil Gibran
The Prophet

Be observant if you would have a pure heart, for something is born to you in consequence of every action.

—Jelaluddin Rumi

If one listens to the faintest but constant suggestions of his genius, which are certainly true, he sees not to what extremes, or even insanity, it may lead him; and yet that way, as he grows more resolute and faithful, his road lies. The faintest assured objection which one healthy man feels will at length prevail over the arguments and customs of mankind. No man ever followed his genius till it misled him.

—Henry David Thoreau

Who is more foolish, the child afraid of the dark or the man afraid of the Light?

—Maurice Freehill

The best guide in life is strength. In religion, as in all other matters, discard everything that weakens you, have nothing to do with it.

—Swami Vivekananda

So the past is not to be wiped away through time. Time is not the way to freedom. Is not this idea of gradualness a form of indolence, of incapacity to deal with the past instantly as it arises? When you have that astonishing capacity to observe clearly as it arises and when you give your mind and heart completely to observe it, then the past ceases. So time and thought do not end the past, for time and thought are the past.

—J. Krishnamurti

Anyone who has ever "gotten it" by following some so-called method, has gotten it in spite of the method, not because of it.

—Lee Lozowick

People think angels fly because they have wings. Angels fly because they take themselves lightly.

—Source unknown

Problems are not problems at all, but results that are dissatisfying.

—Jerry Gillies

I know this, with sure and certain knowledge: a man's work is nothing but this slow trek to rediscover, through the detours of art, those two or three great and simple images in whose presence his heart first opened. This is why, after working and producing for twenty years, I still live with the idea that my work has not even begun.

—Albert Camus

God speaks as softly as He can, and as loudly as He has to.

—Rafi Zabor

Everybody is all right really.

—Winnie the Pooh
A.A. Milne's *Winnie-the-Pooh*

○ ○ ○ ○ ○

The necessary premise is that a man is somehow more than his "characteristics," all the emotions, strivings, tastes, and constructions which it pleases him to call "My Life." We have ground to hope that a Life is something more than a cloud of particles, mere facticity. Go through what is comprehensible and you conclude that only the incomprehensible gives any light.

—Saul Bellow
Herzog

The tendency of an event to occur varies inversely with one's preparation for it.

—David Searls

The only important thing is to follow nature. A tiger should be a good tiger; a tree, a good tree. So man should be man. But to know what man is, one must follow nature and go alone, admitting the importance of the unexpected. Still, nothing is possible without love. . . . For love puts one in a mood to risk everything, and not to withhold important elements.

—Carl Jung

Life is not a series of gig lamps symmetrically arranged; life is a luminous halo, a semi-transparent envelope surrounding us from the beginning of consciousness to the end.

—Virginia Woolf

It is a profitable thing, if one is wise, to seem foolish.

—Aeschylus

The idea is not to become a mere sloth, sitting on your behind with a vacant mind. It is rather to get into the position of being able to concentrate enormously, so that you can, so to speak, look with all your energy—so that you do not miss a thing.

—Paul Weinpahl

What would people think about if they were not taught what to think about?

—Arthur Morgan

There is no use in one person attempting to tell another what the meaning of life is. It involves too intimate an awareness. A major part of the meaning of life is contained in the very discovering of it. It is an ongoing experience of growth that involves a deepening contact with reality. To speak as though it were an objective knowledge, like the date of the war of 1812, misses the point altogether. The meaning of life is indeed objective when it is reached, but the way to it is by a path of subjectivities. . . . The meaning of life cannot be told; it has to happen to a person.

—Ira Progoff

When I was a kid I drew like Michelangelo. It took me years to learn to draw like a kid.

—Pablo Picasso

I have been in love with painting ever since I became conscious of it at the age of six. I drew some pictures I thought fairly good when I was fifty, but really nothing I did before the age of seventy was of any value at all. At seventy-three I have at last caught every aspect of nature—birds, fish, animals, insects, trees, grasses, all. When I am eighty I shall have developed still further, and I will really master the secrets of art at ninety. When I reach a hundred my work will be truly sublime, and my final goal will be attained around the age of one hundred and ten, when every line and dot I draw will be imbued with life.

—Katsushika Hokusai

I remembered one morning when I discovered a cocoon in the bark of a tree, just as the butterfly was making a hole in its case and preparing to come out. I waited a while, but it was too long appearing and I was impatient. I bent over it and breathed on it to warm it. I warmed it as quickly as I could and the miracle began to happen before my eyes, faster than life. The case opened, the butterfly started slowly crawling out, and I shall never forget my horror when I saw how its wings were folded back and crumpled; the wretched butterfly tried with its whole trembling body to unfold them. Bending over it, I tried to help it with my breath. In vain. It needed to be hatched out patiently and the unfolding of the wings needed to be a gradual process in the sun. Now it was too late. My breath had forced the butterfly to appear, all crumpled, before its time. It struggled desperately and, a few seconds later, died in the palm of my hand.

That little body is, I do believe, the greatest weight I have on my conscience. For I realize today that it is a mortal sin to violate the greatest laws of nature. We should not hurry, we should not be impatient, but we should confidently obey the eternal rhythm.

—Nikos Kazantzakis
Zorba The Greek

Let us be kinder to one another.

—Aldous Huxley's last words

To be sighted in the land of the blind carries its own perils. If you try to interpret what you see for the blind, you tend to forget that the blind possess an inherent movement conditioned by their blindness. They are like a monstrous machine moving along its own path. They have their own momentum, their own fixations.

—Frank Herbert
Children Of Dune

Go *with* the pain, let it take you. . . . Open your palms and your body to the pain. It comes in waves like a tide, and you must be open as a vessel lying on the beach, letting it fill you up and then, retreating, leaving you empty and clear. . . . With a deep breath—it has to be as deep as the pain—one reaches a kind of inner freedom from pain, as though the pain were not yours but your body's. The spirit lays the body on the altar.

—Anne Morrow Lindbergh
War Within And Without

It is only the untalented director who imagines himself in every part, wants his own thoughts and emotions portrayed; it is only the untalented who makes his own limitations those of the actor as well.

—Liv Ullmann
Changing

But such is the irresistible nature of truth, that all it asks, and all it wants, is the liberty of appearing.

—Thomas Paine

God, my God, God Whom I meet in darkness, with You it is always the same thing! Always the same question that nobody knows how to answer!

I have prayed to You in the daytime with thoughts and reasons, and in the nighttime You have confronted me, scattering thought and reason. I have come to You in the morning with light and with desire, and You have descended upon me, with great gentleness, with most forbearing silence, in this inexplicable night, dispersing light, defeating all desire. I have explained to You a hundred times my motives for entering the monastery and You have listened and said nothing, and I have turned away and wept with shame.

Is it true that all my motives have meant nothing? Is it true that all my desires were an illusion?

While I am asking questions which You do not answer, You ask me a question which is so simple that I cannot answer. I do not even understand the question.

This night, and every night, it is the same question.

—Thomas Merton
The Sign Of Jonas

I never saw an instance of one or two disputants convincing the other by argument.
—Thomas Jefferson

If you never want to see the face of hell, when you come home from work every night dance with your kitchen towel and, if you're worried about waking up your family, take off your shoes.

—Rabbi Nachman of Bratzlav

○ ○ ○ ○ ○

"I can't believe that," said Alice.

"Can't you?" the Queen said, in a pitying tone. "Try again: draw a long breath and shut your eyes."

Alice laughed. "There's no use trying," she said. "One can't believe impossible things."

"I dare say you haven't had much practice," said the Queen. "When I was younger, I always did it for half an hour a day. Why, sometimes I've believed as many as six impossible things before breakfast."

—Lewis Carroll
Through The Looking Glass

Things that are good are good, and if one is responding to that goodness one is in contact with a truth from which one is getting something. . . . The truth of the sunshine, the truth of the rain, the truth of the fresh air, the truth of the wind in the trees . . . and if we allow ourselves to be benefited by the forms of truth that are readily accessible to us instead of rejecting . . . them as "merely natural" we will be in a better position to profit by higher forms of truth when they come our way.

—Thomas Merton
Contemplation In A World Of Action

He knew that insofar as one denies what is, one is possessed by what is not, the compulsions, the fantasies, the terrors that flock to fill the void.

—Ursula K. LeGuin
The Lathe Of Heaven

The soul is light, the mind is light, and the body is light—light of different grades; it is this relation which connects man with the planets and stars.

—Hazrat Inayat Khan

Actualization of self cannot be sought as a goal in its own right. . . . Rather, it seems to be a by-product of active commitment of one's talents to some cause, outside the self, such as the quest for beauty, truth, or justice.

—Sidney M. Jourard

Of course there's a lot of knowledge in universities. The freshmen bring a little in; the seniors don't take much away; so knowledge sort of accumulates.

—Dr. A. Lawrence Lowell

Everyday happiness means getting up in the morning, and you can't wait to finish your breakfast. You can't wait to do your exercises. You can't wait to put on your clothes. You can't wait to get out—and you can't wait to come home, because the soup is hot.

—George Burns

The bold and handsome young Samurai warrior stood respectfully before the aged Zen master and asked, "Master, teach me about heaven and hell." The master snapped his head up in disgust and said, "Teach YOU about heaven and hell!? Why, I doubt that you could even learn to keep your own sword from rusting! You ignorant fool! How dare you suppose that you could understand anything I might have to say!" The old man went on and on, becoming even more insulting, while the young swordsman's surprise turned first to confusion and then to hot anger, rising by the minute. Master or no master, who can insult a Samurai and live? At last, with teeth clenched and blood nearly boiling in fury, the warrior blindly drew his sword and prepared to end the old man's sharp tongue and life all in a moment. The master looked straight into his eyes and said gently, "That's hell." At the peak of his rage, the Samurai realized that this was indeed his teaching; the Master had hounded him into a living hell, driven by uncontrolled anger and ego. The young man, profoundly humbled, sheathed his sword and bowed low to this great spiritual teacher. Looking up into the wise man's aged, beaming face, he felt more love and compassion than he had ever felt in his life, at which point the master raised his index finger as would a schoolteacher, and said, "And *that's* heaven."

—Source unknown

○ ○ ○ ○ ○

"Maybe you're right, boss. It all depends on the way you look at it. . . . Look, one day I had gone to a little village. An old grandfather of ninety was busy planting an almond tree. 'What, grandad!' I exclaimed. 'Planting an almond tree?' And he, bent as he was, turned

round and said, 'My son, I carry on as if I should never die.' I replied, 'And I carry on as if I was going to die any minute.' Which of us was right, boss?"

—Nikos Kazantzakis
Zorba The Greek

If one changes internally, one should not continue to live with the same objects. They reflect one's mind and psyche of yesterday. I throw away what has no dynamic, living use. I keep nothing to remind me of the passage of time, deterioration, loss, shriveling.

—Anaïs Nin

You want to be loved because you do not love; but the moment you love, it is finished, you are no longer inquiring whether or not somebody loves you.

—J. Krishnamurti

Till the first friend dies, we think ecstasy impersonal, but then discover that he was the cup from which we drank it, itself as yet unknown.

—Emily Dickinson

Don Juan assured me that in order to accomplish the feat of making myself miserable I had to work in a most intense fashion, and that it was absurd. I had now realized I could work just the same in making myself complete and strong. "The trick is in what one emphasizes," he said. "We either make ourselves miserable, or we make ourselves strong. The amount of work is the same."

—Carlos Castaneda
Journey To Ixtlan

Your understandings are of misunderstandings.

—St. Francis

We ourselves feel that what we are doing is just a drop in the ocean. But if that drop was not in the ocean, I think the ocean would be less because of that missing drop. I do not agree with the big way of doing things. To us what matters is the individual. To get to love the person we must come in close contact with him. If we wait till we get the numbers, then we will be lost in the numbers. And we will never be able to show that love and respect for the person. I believe in person to person; every person is Christ for me, and since there is only one Jesus, that person is the one person in the world at that moment.

—Mother Theresa

If anyone says, "I love God," and hates his brother, he is a liar; for he who does not love his brother whom he has seen, cannot love God whom he has not seen.

1 John 4:21

A human being is a part of the whole, called by us the "universe," a part limited in time and space. He experiences himself, his thoughts and feelings, as something separated from the rest— a kind of optical delusion of his consciousness. This delusion is a kind of prison for us, restricting us to our personal desires and to affection for a few persons nearest to us. Our task must be to free ourselves from this prison by widening our circle of compassion to embrace all living creatures and the whole of nature in its beauty.

—Albert Einstein

Enlightened space, the place of unconditional love, cannot be achieved until and unless one is willing to be comfortable with paradox and confusion.

—Ralph Walker

○ ○ ○ ○ ○

Newspapers are unable, seemingly, to discriminate between a bicycle accident and the collapse of civilization.

—George Bernard Shaw

We may be the playthings of fate. We cannot breathe without taking life. As we talk here, we are ourselves the cause of the deaths of countless little lives. We have surely let old bodies go many times, as though changing from old clothes into new ones. We have died more times in the past than all the times we have fallen asleep since being born. . . . Await the time. What use is impatience?

—*The Ramayana*

When anyone seriously pursues an art—painting, poetry, sculpture, composing—over twenty or thirty years, the sustained discipline carries the artist down to the countryside of grief; and that descent, resisted so long, proves invigorating. . . . As I've gotten older, I find I am able to be nourished more by sorrow and to distinguish it from depression.

—Robert Bly

The greatest thing a human being ever does is to see something and tell what he sees in a plain way.

—John Ruskin

To some extent, each of us marries to make up for his own deficiencies. As a child, no one can stand alone against his family and the community, and in all but the most extreme instances, he is in no position to leave and to set up a life elsewhere. In order to survive as children, we have all had to exaggerate those aspects of ourselves that pleased those on whom we depended, and to disown those attitudes and behaviors that were unacceptable to them. As a result, to varying degrees, we have each grown into disproportionate configurations of what we could be as human beings. What we lack, we seek out and then struggle against in those whom we select as mates. We marry the other because he (or she) is different from us, and then we complain, "Why can't he (she) be more like me?"

—Sheldon Kopp
If You Meet The Buddha On The Road, Kill Him

You can be up to your boobies in white satin, with gardenias in your hair and no sugar cane for miles, but you can still be working on a plantation.

—Billie Holiday

We cannot cure the evils of politics with politics. . . . Fifty years ago if we had gone the way of Freud (to study and tackle hostility within ourselves) instead of Marx, we might be closer to peace than we are.

—Anaïs Nin

I'd rather learn from one bird how to sing than to teach ten thousand stars how not to dance.

—ee cummings

O O O O O

Sometimes it seems to me that in this absurdly random life there is some inherent justice in the outcome of personal relationships. In the long run, we get no more than we have been willing to risk giving.

—Sheldon Kopp
If You Meet The Buddha On The Road, Kill Him

This urge to make everything profound. What nonsense!

—Henry Miller

Everyone has talent. What is rare is the courage to follow that "talent" to the dark place where it leads.

—Erica Jong

I am convinced, both by faith and experience, that to maintain one's self on the earth is not a hardship but a pastime—if we live simply and wisely.

—Henry David Thoreau

One has not only an ability to perceive the world but an ability to alter one's perception of it; more simply, one can change things by the manner in which one looks at them.

—Tom Robbins
Even Cowgirls Get The Blues

Have you ever seen an inchworm crawl up a leaf or a twig, and then, clinging to the very end, revolve in the air, feeling for something, to reach something? That's like me. I am trying to find something out there beyond the place on which I have footing.

—Albert P. Ryder

If a little knowledge is dangerous, where is a man who has so much as to be out of danger?

—Thomas Henry Huxley

It is the process of accumulation that creates habit, imitation, and for the mind that accumulates there is deterioration, death. But a mind that is not accumulating, not gathering, that is dying each day, each minute—for such a mind there is no death. It is in a state of infinite space.

So the mind must die to everything it has gathered—to all the habits, the imitated virtues, to all the things it has relied upon for its sense of security. Then it is no longer caught in the net of its own thinking. In dying to the past from moment to moment the mind is made fresh, therefore it can never deteriorate or set in motion the wave of darkness.

—J. Krishnamurti
Think On These Things

I climb the road to Cold Mountain,
The road to Cold Mountain that never ends.
The valleys are long and strewn with stones;
The streams broad and banked with thick grass.
Moss is slippery, though no rain has fallen;
Pines sigh, but it isn't the wind.
Who can break from the snares of the world
And sit with me among the white clouds?

—Han-Shan
Cold Mountain

Here I am, fifty-eight, and I still don't know what I'm going to be when I grow up.

—Peter Drucker

Political language . . . is designed to make lies sound truthful and murder respectable, and to give an appearance of solidity to pure wind.

—George Orwell

Military intelligence is a contradiction in terms.

—Groucho Marx

One sees it as marvelous, another also speaks of it as marvelous, but even after having heard of it, no one whatsoever knows it.

—*Bhagavad Gita*

Finally you understand that the real motorcycle you're working on is yourself.

—Robert M. Pirsig
Zen And The Art Of Motorcycle Maintenance

○ ○ ○ ○ ○

I say that radiation is inherently disintegrative: it comes apart. Gravity is inherently integrative: it pulls together. And to me, there's a good possibility that love is what I'd call metaphysical gravity. It really holds everything together.

—R. Buckminster Fuller

If you wish to make an apple pie from scratch, you must first create the universe.

—Carl Sagan

The world is a looking glass and gives back to every man the reflection of his own face.

—William Makepeace Thackeray

Kinds of cultural change: there is change by necessity, or adaptation, and there is contrived change or novelty.

—Wendell Berry

What is grief compared to physical pain? Whatever fools may say, the body can suffer twenty times more than the mind. The mind has always some power of evasion. At worst, the unbearable thought only comes back and back, but the physical pain can be absolutely continuous. Grief is like a bomber circling round and dropping its bombs each time the circle brings it overhead; physical pain is like the steady barrage on a trench in World War I, hours of it with no letup for a moment. Thought is never static; pain often is.

—C.S. Lewis
A Grief Observed

A happy marriage is the union of two good forgivers.

—Robert Quillen

But what is your duty? The demands of every day.

—Johann Wolfgang von Goethe

○ ○ ○ ○ ○

To a worm in horseradish, the whole world is horseradish.

—Yiddish proverb

A Pentagon official once said the people who would actually push the button probably have never seen a person die. He said the only hope—and it's a strange thought—is if they put the button to launch the nuclear war behind a man's heart. The President, then, with a rusty knife, would have to cut out the man's heart, kill the man, to get to the button.

—Robin Williams

A dog is not considered a good dog because he is a good barker. A man is not considered a good man because he is a good talker.

—Chuang Tzu

I should like to insist that nearly all the important questions, the things we ponder in our profoundest moments, have no answers.

—Jacquetta Hawkes

It is popularly supposed that between those who use the word "God" and those who do not there is a great gulf. But the gulf lies elsewhere. It lies between those who dogmatize, either positively or negatively, and those who recognize in great humility that something within them bears witness to realities which may be momentous in our lives, but which lie beyond the grasping net of our categories of thought.

—Phillip Hewett

In a dream I am walking joyfully up the mountain. Something breaks and falls away, and all is light. Nothing has changed, yet all is amazing, luminescent, free. Released at last, I rise into the sky. . . . This dream comes often. Sometimes I run, then lift up like a kite, high above earth, and always I sail transcendent for a time before awaking. I *choose* to awake, for fear of falling, yet such dreams tell me that I am a part of things, if only I would let go, and keep on going.

In recent dreams, I have twice seen light so brilliant, so intense, that it "woke me up," but the light did not continue into wakefulness. Which was more real, the waking or the dream?

—Peter Matthiesson
Nine-Headed Dragon River

Is sleep a mating with oneself?

—Novalis

Our language has wisely sensed the two sides of being alone. It has created the word "loneliness" to express the pain of being alone. And it has created the word "solitude" to express the glory of being alone.

—Paul Tillich
The Eternal Now

Better to be quarreling than lonesome.

—Irish proverb

At the innermost core of all loneliness is a deep and powerful yearning for union with one's lost self.

—Brendan Francis

Heart, I told you before and twice, and three times, don't knock at that door. No one will answer.

—Spanish folk song

It is a strange feeling—no hopefulness is in it, no despair. Content—that is it; and irresponsibility, but without licentious inclination. I speak now of my profoundest sense of being, not of an incidental feeling.

—Herman Melville

I made connection with a pair of eyes, and I thought, "This is incredible; these eyes are penetrating me." I went through the whole performance just relating to those eyes, giving the whole thing to those eyes. When curtain call finally came, I looked in the direction of those eyes, and it was a seeing eye dog. . . . I couldn't get over it—the compassion and intensity and understanding in those eyes, and it was a dog.

—Al Pacino

Man's mind is a mirror of a universe that mirrors man's mind.

—Joseph Chilton Pearce

True love hurts. It always has to hurt. It must be painful to love someone, painful to leave them, you might have to die for them. When people marry they have to give up everything to love each other. The mother who gives birth to her child suffers much. It is the same for us in the religious life. To belong fully to God we have to give up everything. Only then can we truly love. The word "love" is so misunderstood and so misused.

—Mother Theresa

Three words were in the captain's heart. He shaped them soundlessly with his trembling lips, as he had not breath to spare for a whisper: "I am lost." And, having given up life, the captain suddenly began to live.

—Carson McCullers
Reflections In A Golden Eye

O O O O O

As he told me about his plans, I listened but could not forget that he would not last the week. What folly to be talking of the future, of his future! But once outside, I could not help thinking that after all there is not much difference between a mortal man and a dying man. The absurdity of making plans is only slightly more obvious in the second case.

—E.M. Cioran

The day after tomorrow is the third day of the rest of your life.

—George Carlin

We're all doing time. As soon as we get born, we find ourselves assigned to one little body, one set of desires and fears, one family, city,

state, country, and planet. Who can ever understand exactly why or how it comes down as it does? The bottom line is, here we are. Whatever, wherever, whenever we are, this is what we've got. It's up to us whether we do it as easy time or hard time.

—Bo Lozoff

Ah, the sweet sorrow of loving a parent. It is as pure as the taste of a sourball when you are five.

—Norman Mailer
Tough Guys Don't Dance

I was as sure as that I was alive, that happiness not only needs no justification, but that it is also the only final test of whether what I am doing is right for me. Only of course happiness is not the same as pleasure; it includes the pain of losing as well as the pleasure of finding.

—Joanna Field
A Life Of One's Own

On some hill of despair the bonfire you kindle can light the great sky—though it's true, of course, to make it burn you have to throw yourself in.

—Galway Kinnell

Do you change people first or do you change society? I believe this is a false dichotomy. You have to change both simultaneously. If you're changing only yourself and have no concern for changing the society, something goes awry. If you're changing only society but not changing yourself, something goes awry, as tended to happen in the late 1960s. Now, "simultaneously" may be an overstatement, because I think there are periods when one has to concentrate on one

or the other. And there are periods in a society, in a culture, when the emphasis is appropriate only on one or the other. What I'm trying to say is, never lose sight of either the internal world or the external world, the peace within and the peace based on justice on the outside.

—David Dellinger

The point is to be invisible or blinding, nothing in between.

—Source unknown

Who told you that you were permitted to settle in? Who told you that this or that would last forever? Did no one ever tell you that you will never feel at home in the world?

—Stanislaw Baranczak

In the face of suffering, one has no right to turn away, not to see. In the face of injustice, one may not look the other way. When someone suffers, and it is not you, he comes first. His very suffering gives him priority. . . . To watch over a man who grieves is a more urgent duty than to think of God.

—Elie Wiesel

If we could learn to learn from pain
even as it grasps us. . . .

—Adrienne Rich

Remember this: all suffering comes to an end. And whatever you suffer authentically, God has suffered from it first.

—Meister Eckhart

Do not be afraid.

—Jesus

○ ○ ○ ○ ○

We have to stumble through so much dirt and humbug before we reach home. And we have no one to guide us. Our only guide is our homesickness.

—Hermann Hesse
Steppenwolf

I fear nothing, I hope for nothing, I am free.
—Nikos Kazantzakis

Idealistic reformers are dangerous because their idealism has no roots in love, but is simply a hysterical and unbalanced rage for order amidst their own chaos.

—William Irwin Thompson

When we try to pick out anything by itself, we find it hitched to everything else in the universe.
—John Muir

Find your home in the haunts of every living creature. Make yourself higher than all heights and lower than all depths. Bring together in yourself all opposites of quality: heat and cold, dryness and fluidity. Think that you are everywhere at once, on land, at sea, in heaven. Think that you are not yet begotten, that you are in the womb, that you are young, that you are old, that you have died, that you are in the world beyond the grave. Grasp in your thought all this at once, all times and places, all substances and qualities and magnitudes together. Then you can apprehend God.

—Hermes Trismegistus

She had opened her mind to the words the way an eye used to darkness, veiled with its lashes, opens cautiously to the light, and, finding it even a little blinding, closes itself too late. The light had come, and come invincibly, even after the eye had renounced it. It was too late to unsee.

—Hannah Green
I Never Promised You A Rose Garden

The more a person is able to direct his life consciously, the more he can use time for constructive benefits. The more, however, he is conformist, unfree, undifferentiated, the more, that is, he works not by choice but by compulsion, the more he is then the object of quantitative time. . . . The less alive a person is—"alive" here defined as having conscious direction of his life—the more is time for him the time of the clock. The more alive he is, the more he lives by qualitative time.

—Rollo May

Come, come, whoever you are,
Wanderer, worshipper, lover of leaving—it
　　doesn't matter,
Ours is not a caravan of despair.
Come, even if you have broken your vow a
　　hundred times
Come, come again, come.

—Jelaluddin Rumi

Worse than war is fear of war.
—Lucius Annaeus Seneca

A man must die; that is, he must free himself from a thousand petty attachments and identifications. . . . He is attached to everything in his life, attached to his imagination, attached to his stupidity, attached even to his sufferings, possibly to his sufferings more than to anything else. . . . Attachments to things, identifications with things, keep alive a thousand useless "I"s in a man. These "I"s must die in order that the big I may be born. But how can they be made to die? They do not want to die. It is at this point that the possibility of awakening comes to the rescue. To awaken means to realize one's nothingness.

—G.I. Gurdjieff

Sharp nostalgia, infinite and terrible, for what I already possess.

—Juan Ramon Jimenez

All disciples are idiots. What were Tolstoy's followers? What are the Marxists? What are the Chassidim who wrangle and push to pick up the holy crumbs from the rabbi's banquet? What are those would-be artists who imitate Picasso or Chagall? They're a flock of sheep, and they're always driven by a dog.

—Isaac Bashevis Singer

If you want to know the taste of a pear, you must change the pear by eating it yourself.

—Mao Tse Tung

It's not the length but the quality of life that matters to me. It has always been important to me to write one sentence at a time, to live every day as if it were my last and judge it in those terms, often badly, not because it lacked grand gesture or grand passion but because it failed in the daily virtues of self-discipline, kindness, and laughter. It is love, very ordinary, human love, and not fear, which is the good teacher and the wisest judge.

—Jane Rule

A hundred times every day I remind myself that my inner and outer life depends on the labors of other men, living and dead, and that I must exert myself in order to give in the measure as I have received and am still receiving.

—Albert Einstein

It seems to me like this. It's not a terrible thing —I mean it may be terrible, but it's not damaging, it's not poisoning to do without something one really wants. . . . What's terrible is to pretend that the second-rate is first-rate. To pretend that you don't need love when you do; or you like your work when you know quite well you're capable of better.

—Doris Lessing

Love is not consolation, it is light.

—Simone Weil

A Twentieth Century-Fox executive in Paris arranged for an exhibit of the fake paintings used in the movie "How To Steal A Million." He phoned Howard Newman of the New York office, who said the fakes could not be shipped because they were on tour. "What should I do?" asked the Paris man frantically. "Get some originals," said Newman. "Nobody'll know the difference."

—Richard Kehl
Silver Departures

The foot feels the foot when it feels the ground.

—Buddha

○ ○ ○ ○ ○

People think love is an emotion. Love is good sense.

—Ken Kesey

Not equal to
Not metaphor
Not standing for
Not sign.

—Minor White

One can give nothing whatever without giving oneself—that is to say, risking oneself. If one cannot risk oneself, then one is simply incapable of giving.

—James Baldwin
The Fire Next Time

Very seldom will a person give up on himself. He continues to have hope because he knows he has the potential for change. He tries again —not just to exist, but to bring about those changes in himself that will make his life worth living. Yet people are very quick to give up on friends, and especially on their spouses, to declare them hopeless, and to either walk away or do nothing more than resign themselves to a bad situation.

—Hugh Prather
Notes On Love And Courage

Everybody's looking for the man on the white horse, everybody's looking for the one who will tell the Truth. So you read Lao-tzu, you read Konrad Lorenz, I don't know who else, Melville, Kenneth Patchen, somebody you think is not a bullshitter. Somebody who has the eyes of a saint and the perceptions of a ghost.

They're gonna tell us the way, they're gonna show us. They never really do, and we run around being cheap imitations of all those influences.

—Marlon Brando
interviewed in *Rolling Stone*, May 1976

Even monkeys fall out of trees.

—Japanese proverb

When you talk about Jung's ideas, it's important never to say the phrase "collective unconscious." That's his phrase. You must make up one for the same experience. Call it "the great lake." If you're an earth type, call it "the granite magma layer." If you're an air type, call it "the beehive of thoughts." Ask your own psyche to rise, and slowly eat the phrase, and change it as it wishes. The problem of your own originality will then arise. If instead of "collective unconscious," you say "beehive of thoughts," you'll notice that the concept you've expressed is already different from the concept "the collective unconscious." Then you are responsible for that difference. You'd better be ready to defend it.

If we all did that, we'd see less of the goo that we constantly see in spiritual magazines. The word "bliss" appears again and again. "Bliss" means absolutely nothing. I have never met an American who felt "bliss." The whole move-

ment is penetrated by catch phrases. . . . The political movement of the Sixties died because people accepted the language without changing it. The Marxists accepted Marx's language, the students accepted hippie language, the love generation accepted jazz musician's language. . . . Language is important. . . . If, as in the English department, the language is all received knowledge that the psyche has not absorbed and interpenetrated, then the language is dead. . . .

—Robert Bly
EastWest Journal, August 1976

You have to go beyond words and conceptualized ideas and just get into what you are, deeper and deeper. The first glimpse is not quite enough; you have to examine the details without judging, without using words and concepts. Opening to oneself fully is opening to the world.

—Chögyam Trungpa
Cutting Through Spiritual Materialism

I say you shall yet find the
friend you were looking for.

—Walt Whitman

Truth is error burned up.

—Norman O. Brown

That's the way it is.

—Walter Cronkite

○ ○ ○ ○ ○

If there is a sin against life, it consists perhaps not so much in despairing of life as in hoping for another life and in eluding the implacable grandeur of this life.

—Albert Camus

The most beautiful music of all is the music of what happens.

—Irish proverb

It is in affliction itself that the splendor of God's mercy shines, from its very depths, in the heart of its inconsolable bitterness. If still persevering in our love, we fall to the point where the soul cannot keep back the cry, "My God, why hast thou forsaken me?", if we remain at this point without ceasing to love, we end by touching something that is not affliction, not joy, an essence, necessary and pure, something not of the senses, common to joy and sorrow: the very love of God.

—Simone Weil

Sad soul, take comfort, nor forget that sunrise never failed us yet.

—Celia Layton Thaxter

A man can no more diminish God's glory by refusing to worship him than a lunatic can put out the sun by scribbling "darkness" on the walls of his cell.

—C.S. Lewis

The purpose is to identify not with the body which is falling away, but with the consciousness of which it is a vehicle. This is something I learned from my myths. Am I the bulb that carries the light, or am I the light of which the bulb is the vehicle? If you can identify with the consciousness, you can watch this thing go like an old car. There goes the fender, etc. But it's expected; and then gradually the whole thing drops off and consciousness rejoins consciousness. I live with these myths—and they tell me to do this, to identify with the Christ or the Shiva in me. And that doesn't die, it resurrects. It is an essential experience of any mystical realization that you die to your flesh and are born to your spirit. You identify with the consciousness in life—and that is the god.

—Joseph Campbell

Conclusions arrived at through reasoning have very little or no influence in altering the course of our lives.

—Carlos Castaneda
The Fire From Within

Does one's integrity ever lie in what he is not able to do? I think that usually it does, for free will does not mean one will, but many wills conflicting in one man. Freedom cannot be conceived simply.

—Flannery O'Connor
Wise Blood

O O O O O

We are most asleep when awake.

—Paul Reps

Tell me to what you pay attention and I will tell you who you are.

—José Ortega y Gasset

Our minds want clothes as much as our bodies.

—Samuel Butler

I have come one step away from everything. And here I stay, far from everything, one step away.

—Antonio Porchia

Her theme was happiness: what it was; what it was not; where we might find it, where not; and how, if found, it must be guarded. Never must we confound it with pleasure. Nor think sorrow its exact opposite.

—Mary Lavin

As you look at many people's lives, you see that their suffering is in a way gratifying, for they are comfortable in it. They make their lives a living hell, but a familiar one.

—Ram Dass
Journey Of Awakening

The ego, as a collection of our past experiences, is continually offering miserable lines of thought. It's as if there were a stream with little fish swimming by, and when we hook one of them there is a judgement. The ego is constantly judging everybody and everything. It has its constant little chit chat about things that can happen in the future, things about the past, too, and these are the little fish that swim by. And what we learn to do—this is why it takes work—is not to reach out and grab a fish, you see.

—Hugh Prather

For the good man to realize that it is better to be whole than to be good is to enter on a

straight and narrow path compared to which his previous rectitude was flowery license.

—John Middleton Murray

Most people really believe that the Christian commandments (e.g., to love one's neighbor as oneself) are intentionally a little too severe— like putting the clock ahead half an hour to make sure of not being late in the morning.

—Sören Kierkegaard

Recently my fingers have developed a prejudice against comparatives. They all follow this pattern: a squirrel is smaller than a tree; a bird is more musical than a tree. Each of us is the strongest one in his own skin. Characteristics should take off their hats to one another, instead of spitting in each other's faces.

—Bertolt Brecht

All that we do
Is touched with ocean, yet we remain
On the shore of what we know.

—Richard Wilbur

There once was a man who cried every time it snowed. He went to a psychotherapist. Now when the snow falls, he weeps for his mother, who died in the winter.

—Joe Riener

○ ○ ○ ○ ○

The family is a good institution because it is uncongenial. The men and women who, for good reasons and bad, revolt against the family, are, for good reasons and bad, revolting against mankind. Aunt Elizabeth is unreasonable, like mankind. Papa is excitable, like mankind. Our younger brother is mischievous, like mankind. Grandpapa is stupid, like the world; he is old, like the world.

—G.K. Chesterton

Great loves too must be endured.

—Coco Chanel

Love is an ideal thing, marriage is a real thing; a confusion of the real with the ideal never goes unpunished.

—Johann Wolfgang von Goethe

Needn't be anything elaborate, he said. Echoes will be fine.

—Richard Kehl

While I generally find that great myths are great precisely because they represent and embody great universal truths, the myth of romantic love is a dreadful lie. Perhaps it is a necessary lie in that it ensures the survival of the falling-in-love experience that traps us into marriage. But as a psychiatrist I weep in my heart almost daily for the ghastly confusion and suffering that this myth fosters. Millions of people waste vast amounts of energy desperately and futilely attempting to make the reality of their lives conform to the unreality of the myth.

—M. Scott Peck

And when will there be an end of marrying? I suppose, when there is an end of living.

—Quintus Tertullian

And as we stray further from love we multiply the words. Had we remained together we could have become a silence.

—Yehuda Amichai

Her hearing was keener than his, and she heard silences he was unaware of.

—D.M. Thomas

Love, all alike, no season knows, nor clime, Nor hours, days, months, which are the rags of time.

—John Donne

Solitude, my mother, tell me my life again.

—O.V. de L. Milosz

If you are afraid of loneliness, don't marry.

—Anton Chekhov

To marry a woman with any success a man must have a total experience of her, he must come to see her and accept her in time as well as in space. Besides coming to love what she is now, he must also come to realize and love equally the baby and the child she once was, and the middle-aged woman and the old crone she will eventually become.

—James Keyes
Only Two Can Play This Game

And it is always the same confession, the same youth, the same pure eyes, the same ingenuous gesture of her arms around my neck, the same caress, the same revelation. But it is never the same woman. The cards have said that I would meet her in life, but without recognizing her.

—Paul Eluard

Chains do not hold a marriage together. It is threads, hundreds of tiny threads which sew people together through the years. That is what makes a marriage last—more than passion or even sex.

—Simone Signoret

The maxim for any love affair is "Play and pray, but on the whole do not pray when you are playing and do not play when you are praying." We cannot yet manage such simultaneities.

—Charles Williams

The reality is that all relationships inevitably will be dissolved and broken. The ultimate price exacted for commitment to other human beings rests in the inescapable fact that loss and pain will be experienced when they are gone, even to the point of jeopardizing one's physical health. It is a toll that no one can escape, and a price that everyone will be forced to pay repeatedly. Like the rise and fall of the ocean tides, disruptions of human relationships occur at regular intervals throughout life, and include the loss of parents, death of a mate, divorce, marital separation, death of family members, children leaving home, death of close friends, change of neighborhoods, and loss of acquaintances by retirement from work. Infancy, adolescence, middle age, old age—all seasons of life involve human loss.

—James J. Lynch

○ ○ ○ ○ ○

The political campaign won't tire me, for I have an advantage. I can be myself.

—John F. Kennedy

Only twice comes that cry of the mother which one hears as without one's self—at birth and at death . . . why the same? Since one is the cry of supreme joy and the other of sorrow . . . is it not that in all the Universe there is but one great continuing Sorrow, Joy, Ecstasy, Agony— the Mother Cry of Creation.

—Isadora Duncan

The white man knows how to make everything, but he does not know how to distribute it.

—Sitting Bull

Jesus Christ is the only God. And so am I. And so are you.

—William Blake

True holiness consists in doing God's will with a smile.

—Mother Theresa

To raise an infant, to look after it, to educate it, and to give oneself to its service is as much and as good as the work of an adept because an adept forgets himself in meditation and a mother forgets herself by giving her life to the child.

—Hazrat Inayat Khan

As you think, you travel. As you love, you attract. You are today where your thoughts have brought you; you will be tomorrow where your thoughts take you. You cannot escape the result of your thoughts; but you can endure and learn, accept and be glad. You will realize the vision of your heart, not the idle wish. You will gravitate toward that which you secretly most love. Into your hands will be placed the exact result of your thoughts; you will receive that which you earn; no more, no less. Whatever your present environment may be, you will fall, remain, or rise with your thoughts, your vision—your ideal.

—Source unknown

What you deny to others will be denied to you, for the plain reason that you are always legislating for yourself, all your words and actions define the world you want to live in.

—Thaddeus Golas
The Lazy Man's Guide To Enlightenment

Loneliness is necessary for pure poetry. When someone intrudes into the poet's life (and any sudden personal contact, whether in the bed or in the heart, is an intrusion) he loses his balance for a moment, slips into being who he is, uses his poetry as one would use money or sympathy. The person who writes the poetry emerges, tentatively, like a hermit crab from a conch shell. The poet, for that instant, ceases to be a dead man.

—Jack Spicer

I beseech you, in the bowels of Christ, think it possible you may be mistaken.

—Oliver Cromwell

○ ○ ○ ○ ○

Anna was saying to herself: why do I always have this awful need to make other people see things as I do? It's childish, why should they? What it amounts to is that I'm scared of being alone in what I feel.

—Doris Lessing
The Golden Notebook

. . . we die to each other daily.
What we know of other people
Is only our memory of the moments
During which we knew them. And they have
    changed since then.
To pretend that they and we are the same
Is a useful and convenient social convention
Which must sometimes be broken. We must
    also remember
That at every meeting we are meeting a
    stranger.

—T.S. Eliot
The Cocktail Party

Each man takes care that his neighbor shall not cheat him. But a day comes when he begins to care that he does not cheat his neighbor. Then all goes well. He has changed his market-cart into a chariot of the sun.

—Ralph Waldo Emerson
Worship

I know a lot of men who are healthier at age fifty than they've ever been before, because a lot of their fear is gone.

—Robert Bly

History is merely a list of surprises. . . . It can only prepare us to be surprised yet again.

—Kurt Vonnegut, Jr.

Millions of persons long for immortality who do not know what to do with themselves on a rainy afternoon.

—Susan Ertz

O my soul, do not aspire to immortal life, but exhaust the limits of the possible.

—Pindar

Where would the gardener be if there were no more weeds?

—Chuang Tzu

○ ○ ○ ○ ○

I don't like work—no man does—but I like what is in work: the chance to find yourself.

—Joseph Conrad
The Heart Of Darkness

The sun will set without thine assistance.

—*The Talmud*

When an apprentice gets hurt, or complains of being tired, the workmen and peasants have this fine expression: "It is the trade entering his body." Each time that we have some pain to go through, we can say to ourselves quite truly that it is the universe, the order and beauty of the world, and the obedience of God that are entering our body.

—Simone Weil
Waiting For God

A young student went to a Sufi teacher and asked, "I have heard that the way of the West is communion with God, and the way of the East is union with God. Can you explain which way is higher?"

"My friend," the Sufi explained, "when there are two airplanes in the air, one at twenty thousand feet, and the other at ten thousand feet, and you are on the ground, what difference does it make to you which is higher?"

—Source unknown

Just because everything is different doesn't mean anything has changed.

—Irene Poter

Men substitute tradition for the living experience of the love of God. They talk and think as though walking with God was attained by walking in the footsteps of men who walked with God.

—Francis Howgill

To be sure, our mental processes often go wrong, so that we imagine God to have gone away. What should be done then? Do exactly what you would do if you felt most secure. Learn to behave thus even in deepest distress and keep yourself that way in any and every estate of life. I can give you no better advice than to find God where you lost him.

—Meister Eckhart

Call it a dream. It does not change anything.

—Ludwig Wittgenstein

I have a good friend, Rudolf Serkin, the pianist, a very sensitive man. I was talking to him one day backstage after a concert and I told him that I thought he had played particularly sensitively that day. I said, "You know, many pianists are brilliant, they strike the keys so well, but somehow you are different." "Ah," he said, "I don't think you should ever strike a key. You should pull the keys with your fingers."

—Andrew Wyeth

It is a great obstacle to happiness to expect too much.

—Bernard de Fontenelle

There should be less talk. A preaching point is not a meeting point.

—Mother Theresa

○ ○ ○ ○ ○

If error is corrected whenever it is recognized as such, the path of error is the path of truth.

—Hans Reichenbach

Coincidence, if traced far enough back, becomes inevitable.

—Hineu

The truth is more important than the facts.

—Frank Lloyd Wright

To love the truth is to refuse to let oneself be saddened by it.

—André Gide

I never give them hell. I just tell the truth and they think it's hell.

—Harry S. Truman

Why is it that reality, when set down untransposed in a book, sounds false?

—Simone Weil

Truth is a river that is always splitting up into arms that reunite. Islanded between the arms, the inhabitants argue for a lifetime as to which is the main river.

—Cyril Connolly

The situation reached the height of the ludicrous when I suddenly realized one day that of everything I had written about the man I could just as well have said the opposite. I had indubitably reached that dead end which lies so artfully hidden in the phrase "the meaning of meaning."

—Henry Miller

An ideal map would contain the map of the map, the map of the map of the map . . . endlessly.

—Alfred Korzybski

Suppose someone claimed to have a microscopically exact replica (in marble, even) of Michelangelo's David in his home. When you go to see this marvel, you find a twenty-foot-tall, roughly rectilinear hunk of pure white marble standing in his living room. "I haven't gotten around to *unpacking* it yet," he says, "but I know it's in there."

—Douglas Hofstadter

I thought we were above questions of good and evil. I am not saying you are bad. That does not concern me. I am saying only that you are *false* with me.

—Anaïs Nin

You have to be true to yourself, but you have to be true to your best self, not to the self that secretly thinks you are better than other people.

—Stephen Gaskin

The most dangerous man in the world is the contemplative who is guided by nobody. He trusts his own visions. He obeys the attractions of an interior voice, but will not listen to other men. He identifies the will of God with anything that makes him feel, within his own heart, a big, warm, sweet interior glow. The sweeter and the warmer the feeling, the more he is convinced of his own infallibility. And if the sheer force of his own self-confidence communicates itself to other people and gives them the impression that he really is a saint, such a man can wreck a whole city or a religious order or even a nation. The world is covered with scars that have been left in its flesh by visionaries like these.

—Thomas Merton

In relief, in humiliation, in terror, he understood that he, too, was an appearance—that someone else was dreaming him.

—Jorge Luis Borges

The honest liar is the man who tells the truth about his old lies; who says on Wednesday, "I told a magnificent lie on Monday."

—G.K. Chesterton

Remember: one lie does not cost you one truth but the truth.

—Friedrich Hebbel

Everything should be as simple as it is, but not simpler.

—Albert Einstein

○ ○ ○ ○ ○

We live on the brink of disaster because we do not know how to let life alone. We do not respect the living and fruitful contradictions and paradoxes of which true life is full.

—Thomas Merton

There is no such thing as chance; and that which seems to us blind accident actually stems from the deepest source of all.

—Friedrich von Schiller

No one ever told us we had to study our lives, make of our lives a study, as if learning natural history or music, that we should begin with the simple exercises first and slowly go on trying the hard ones, practicing till the strength and accu-

racy became one with the daring to leap into transcendence, take the chance of breaking down in the wild arpeggio or faulting the full sentence of the fugue. . . . And in fact we can't live like that: we take on everything at once before we've even begun to read or mark time, we're forced to begin in the midst of the hardest movement, the one already sounding as we are born. . . .

—Adrienne Rich
The Dream Of A Common Language

The moment one gives close attention to anything, even a blade of grass, it becomes a mysterious, awesome, indescribably magnificent world in itself.

—Henry Miller

To punish me for my contempt for authority, fate made me authority myself.

—Albert Einstein

Society highly values its normal man. It educates children to lose themselves and to become absurd, and thus be normal. Normal men have killed perhaps 100,000,000 of their fellow normal men in the last fifty years.

—R.D. Laing

All the archaic images are surfacing out of the collective unconscious. The ancient ways and ancient esoteric schools have taken on a new life in the midst of a technological society. From Tibet, from the Middle East, from Scotland, from Mexico, and from the American Southwest, the archaic ways are coming back and offering themselves to us. They have lived in secret for a long time, and in secrecy they have flourished. Now, as they blaze forth into the open, they will die and, in their death, make a new life possible. Like a dying star that in its explosive end scatters the material needed for the evolution of life, the supernova of the esoteric and occult we are witnessing is both an end and a beginning.

—William Irwin Thompson

You are merely the lens in the beam. You can only receive, give, and possess the light as the lens does.

If you seek yourself, "your rights," you prevent the oil and air from meeting in the flame, you rob the lens of its transparency. . . . You will know life and be acknowledged by it according to your degree of transparency, your capacity, that is, to vanish as an end, and remain purely as a means.

—Dag Hammarskjöld

You may study with the highest teachers, but you will find no one but yourself teaching you. You may travel the world over, yet find nothing but yourself, reflected the world over. So if you now find yourself in a cell, take heart that out of all the teachers in the world, out of all the places in the world, you still have with you the only ultimate ingredient of your journey: yourself.

—Bo Lozoff

For one human being to love another: that is perhaps the most difficult of all our tasks; the ultimate, the last test and proof, the work for which all other work is but preparation.

—Rainer Maria Rilke

○ ○ ○ ○ ○

Spontaneity (the impulses from our best self) gets confused with implusivity and acting-out (the impulses from our sick self) and there is then no way to tell the difference.

—Abraham Maslow

Only the man who can consciously assent to the power of the inner voice becomes a personality.

—Carl Jung

I don't want you to follow me or anyone else. I would not lead you into the promised land if I could, because if I could lead you in, somebody else would lead you out.

—Eugene V. Debs

Whatever has form is in the process still of being formed. Form is never fixed.

—M.C. Richards

Invest in the "process" rather than the product. Process living neutralizes the depleting and impoverishing effects of chronically living in anticipation. Even when impossible goals occasionally are reached, satisfactions derived from them are invariably disappointing unless *the process* has given ample satisfaction along the way.

—Theodore Rubin

A wind blew, from what quarter I know not, but it lifted the half-grown leaves so that there was a flash of silver gray in the air. It was the time between the lights when colors undergo their intensification and purples and golds burn

in windowpanes like the beat of an excitable heart; when for some reason the beauty of the world revealed and yet soon to perish . . . has two edges, one of laughter, one of anguish, cutting the heart asunder.

—Virginia Woolf
A Room Of One's Own

God will invade. But I wonder whether people who ask God to interfere openly and directly in our world quite realize what it will be like when He does. When that happens, it is the end of the world. When the author walks onto the stage the play is over. God is going to invade, all right: but what is the good of saying you are on His side then, when you see the whole natural universe melting away like a dream and something else—something it never entered your head to conceive—comes crashing in; something so beautiful to some of us and so terrible to others that none of us will have any choice left?

—C.S. Lewis

Creativity is not infinite; analysis is.

—David Searls

○ ○ ○ ○ ○

Do not think you will necessarily be aware of your own enlightenment.

—Dogen

We ourselves cannot put any magic spells on this world. The world is its own magic.

—Suzuki Roshi

If you write for God you will reach many men and bring them joy.

If you write for men you may make some money and you may give someone a little joy and you may make a noise in the world, for a little while.

If you write for yourself you can read what you yourself have written and after ten minutes you will be so disgusted you will wish that you were dead.

—Thomas Merton
Seeds Of Contemplation

The application of this knife, the division of the world into parts and the building of this structure, is something everybody does. All the time we are aware of millions of things around us—these changing shapes, these burning hills, the sound of the engine, the feel of the throttle, each rock and weed and fence post and piece of debris beside the road—aware of these things but not really conscious of them unless there is something unusual or unless they reflect something we are predisposed to see. We couldn't possibly be conscious of these things and remember all of them because our mind would be so full of useless details we would be unable to think. From all this awareness we must select, and what we select and call consciousness is never the same as the awareness because the process of selection mutates it. We take a handful of sand from the endless landscape of awareness around us and call that handful of sand the world.

—Robert M. Pirsig
Zen And The Art Of Motorcycle Maintenance

"Oh, if only it were possible to find understanding," Joseph exclaimed. "If only there were a dogma to believe in. Everything is contradictory, everything tangential; there are no certainties anywhere. Everything can be interpreted one way and then again interpreted in the opposite sense. The whole of world history can be explained as development and progress and can also be seen as nothing but decadence and meaninglessness. Isn't there any truth? Is there no real and valid doctrine?"

The Master had never heard him speak so fervently. He walked on in silence for a little, then said, "There is truth, my boy. But the doctrine you desire, absolute, perfect dogma that alone provides wisdom, does not exist. Nor should you long for a perfect doctrine, my friend. Rather, you should long for the perfection of yourself. The deity is within *you*, not in ideas and books. Truth is lived, not taught. Be prepared for conflicts, Joseph Knecht—I can see they have already begun."

—Hermann Hesse
Magister Ludi (The Glass Bead Game)

I see two birds in the same branch—one eats the sweet fruit, one looks on sadly.

The first bird wonders: in what prison does he live?

The second marvels: how can he rejoice?
—*The Ramayana*

Peace is such a precious jewel that I would give anything for it but truth.

—Matthew Henry

○ ○ ○ ○ ○

Watching a bird makes me feel good. You know that if I were reincarnated, I'd want to come back a buzzard. Nothing hates him or envies him or wants him or needs him. He is never bothered or in danger, and he can eat anything.
—William Faulkner

We are not miserable without feeling it. A ruined house is not miserable.

—Blaise Pascal

What is one to do on a bleak day but drift for a while through the streets—drift with the stream.

—Dag Hammarskjöld

Not to call a thing good a day longer or a day earlier than it seems good to us is the only way to remain really happy.

—Friedrich Nietzsche

If we are suffering illness, poverty, or misfortune, we think we shall be satisfied on the day it ceases. But there, too, we know it is false; so soon as one has got used to not suffering one wants something else.

—Simone Weil

Was then not all sorrow in time, all self-torment and fear in time? Were not all difficulties and evil in the world conquered as soon as one conquered time, as soon as one dispelled time?

—Hermann Hesse
Siddhartha

Politics, as hopeful men practice it in the world, consists mainly of the delusion that a change in form is a change in substance.

—H.L. Mencken

A person who believes, as she did, that things fit: that there is a whole of which one is a part, and that in being a part one is whole: such a person has no desire whatever, at any time, to play God. Only those who have denied their being yearn to play at it.

—Ursula K. LeGuin
The Lathe Of Heaven

The first step . . . shall be to lose the way.
—Galway Kinnell

We begin to realize that there is a sane, awake quality within us. In fact this quality manifests itself only in the absence of struggle. So we discover the Third Noble Truth, the truth of the goal: that is, non-striving. We need only drop the effort to secure and solidify ourselves and the awakened state is present. But we soon realize that just "letting go" is only possible for short periods. We need some discipline to bring us to "letting be." We must walk a spiritual path. Ego must wear itself out like an old shoe, journeying from suffering to liberation.

—Chögyam Trungpa
Cutting Through Spiritual Materialism

Look for a long time at what pleases you, and longer still at what pains you.

—Colette

O O O O O

People say that what we're all seeking is a meaning for life. I don't think that's what we're really seeking. I think that what we're really seeking is an experience of being alive, so that our life experiences on the purely physical plane will have resonances within our innermost being and reality, so that we can actually feel the rapture of being alive.

—Joseph Campbell
The Power Of Myth

Contempt is the weapon of the weak and a defense against one's own despised and unwanted feelings.

—Alice Miller

Why should we honor those that die upon the field of battle? A man may show as reckless courage in entering into the abyss of himself.

—William Butler Yeats

Try? There *is* no try. There is only do or do not do.

—Yoda
"The Empire Strikes Back"

O O O O O

Behind joy and laughter there may be a temperament, coarse, hard, and callous. But behind sorrow there is always sorrow. Pain, unlike pleasure, wears no mask.

—Oscar Wilde

There is the Hindu story of the child in the womb who sang, "Let me remember who I am."

And his first cry after birth was, "Oh, I have forgotten."

—Source unknown

A man has many skins in himself, covering the depths of his heart. Man knows so many things; he does not know himself. Why, thirty or forty skins or hides, just like an ox's or a bear's, so thick and hard, cover the soul. Go into your own ground and learn to know yourself there.

—Meister Eckhart

Most of us do not like to look inside ourselves for the same reason we don't like to open a letter that has bad news.

—Fulton J. Sheen

Life is a rock. And a hard place.

—Juli Duncan

I think we ought to read only the kind of books that wound and stab us. . . . We need the books that affect us like a disaster, that grieve us deeply, like the death of someone we loved more than ourselves, like being banished into forests far from everyone, like a suicide. A book must be the ax for the frozen sea inside us.

—Franz Kafka

It took me fifteen years to discover that I had no talent for writing, but I couldn't give it up because by that time I was too famous.

—Robert Charles Benchley

Every time she passed a mirror she was unable to resist the temptation of looking at the one thing that interested her most in the world—herself. And every time she was a bit disap-pointed—almost as if the girl facing her were some other person.

—Orianna Fallaci
Penelope At War

It is a terrible thing
To be so open: it is as if my heart
Put on a face and walked into the world. . . .
Sylvia Plath
"A Poem For Three Voices"

In our sleep, pain that cannot forget falls drop by drop upon the heart, and in our own despair, against our will, comes wisdom through the awful grace of God.

—Aeschylus

○ ○ ○ ○ ○

Life is a maze in which we take the wrong turn before we have learned to walk.

—Cyril Connolly

Three kinds of souls, three prayers:

1. I am a bow in your hands, Lord. Draw me, lest I rot.

2. Do not overdraw me, Lord. I shall break.

3. Overdraw me, Lord, and who cares if I break!
—Nikos Kazantzakis
Report To Greco

On the mountains of truth you can never climb in vain: either you will reach a point higher up

today, or you will be training your powers so that you will be able to climb higher tomorrow.
—Friedrich Nietzsche

He led a double life. Did that make him a liar? He did not feel a liar. He was a man of two truths.
—Iris Murdoch

May my silences become more accurate.
—Theodore Roethke

Only to have a grief
equal to all these tears!

—Adrienne Rich

I don't know what your destiny will be, but one thing I do know: the only ones among you who will be really happy are those who have sought and found how to serve.
—Albert Schweitzer

No trace: when you do something, you should burn yourself completely, like a good bonfire, leaving no trace of yourself.
—Suzuki Roshi

Life does not need to mutilate itself in order to be pure.

—Simone Weil

To stand on one leg and prove God's existence is a very different thing from going down on one's knees and thanking him.
—Sören Kierkegaard

He who believes in nothing still needs a girl to believe in him.
—Eugene Rosenstock-Huessy

Just remember, we're all in this alone.
—Lily Tomlin

The one who praises you is a thief. The one who criticizes you is your true friend.
—Seung Sahn

The problem with introducing Oriental spirituality into America today is that the cultural barrier which the light from the East must pass through functions as a thick prism. The prism consists of American consumer culture and psychological individualism. Robbed by the prism of its color and sharpness, the now-refracted Oriental light serves as one more support for the structure its original teachers had most hoped it would undermine: the isolated, Western competitive ego.

—Harvey Cox

No snowflake ever falls in the wrong place.
—Zen saying

○ ○ ○ ○ ○

The contrast between that bright blue and white Christmas-tree ornament and the black sky, that infinite universe, and the size and significance of it really comes through. It is so small and so fragile, such a precious little spot in that universe, that you can block it out with your thumb. You realize that everything that means anything to you—all of history and art and death and birth and love, tears and joys, all of it, is on that little blue and white spot out there which you can cover with your thumb.

And you realize from that perspective that you have changed, that there is something new, that the relationship is no longer what it was.

—Astronaut Russell Schweickart

Once in ancient India there was a tournament held to test marksmanship in archery. A wooden fish was set up on a high pole and the eye of the fish was the target. One by one many valiant princes came and tried their skill, but in vain. Before each one shot his arrow the teacher asked him what he saw, and invariably all replied that they saw a fish on a pole at a great height with head, eyes, etc.; but Arjuna, as he took his aim, said, "I see the eye of the fish," and he was the only one who succeeded in hitting the mark.

—Paramananda

You cannot stay on the summit forever; you have to come down again. . . . So why bother in the first place? Just this: what is above knows what is below, but what is below does not know what is above.

One climbs, one sees. One descends, one sees no longer but one has seen. There is an art to conducting oneself in the lower regions by the memory of what one saw higher up. When one can no longer see, one can at least still know.

—Rene Daumal
Mount Analogue

The transmigration of life takes place in one's mind. Let one therefore keep the mind pure, for what a man thinks, that he becomes.

—*The Upanishads*

It is a terrible thing, this kindness that human beings do not lose. Terrible because when we are finally naked in the dark and cold, it is all we have. We who are so rich, so full of strength, wind up with that small change. We have nothing else to give.

—Ursula K. LeGuin

Freedom breeds freedom. Nothing else does.

—Anne Roe

○ ○ ○ ○ ○

When I pray, I never pray for myself, always for others, or else I hold a silly, naive, or deadly serious dialogue with what is deepest inside me, which for the sake of convenience I call God. Praying to God for something for yourself strikes me as being too childish for words. To pray for another's well-being is something I find childish as well; one should only pray that another should have enough strength to shoulder his burden. If you do that, you lend him some of your own strength.

—Etty Hillesum
An Interrupted Life

A garden I tend whose blossom never existed.

—Pablo Neruda

I remember hearing years ago that there was a big Hollywood film about the life of Christ being made in Rome. They were shooting the Last Supper, and the director came on the set ready to shoot, and he looked up and there was Christ in the middle and the apostles sitting around the table, and the director started yelling, "Where's John the Baptist?" A very embarrassed assistant director said, "Excuse me, John the Baptist wasn't in the Last Supper." And the director went purple with rage, saying, "When I'm asking where he *is*, I don't want to be told where he *isn't*." How deep-rooted our perceptions can be.

—Peter Brook

I begin with what was always gone.

—M.S. Merwin

Children seldom have a proper sense of their own tragedy, discounting and keeping hidden the true horrors of their short lives, humbly imagining real calamity to be some prestigious drama of the grown-up world.

—Shirley Hazzard

The afternoon knows what the morning never suspected.

—Swedish proverb

We must cultivate and defend particularity, individuality, and irregularity—life. Human beings do not have a future in the collectivism of bureaucratic states or in the mass society created by capitalism. Every system, by virtue as much of its abstract nature as of its pretension to totality, is the enemy of life. As a forgotten Spanish poet, José Moreno Villa, put it with melancholy wit: "I have discovered in symmetry the root of much iniquity."

—Octavio Paz

The way out is through the door you came in.

—R.D. Laing

More than any other time in history, mankind faces the crossroads. One path leads to despair and utter hopelessness, the other to total extinction. I pray we have the wisdom to choose wisely.

—Woody Allen

I have never met anybody who wasn't against war. Even Hitler and Mussolini were, according to themselves.

—David Low

Disbelief in magic can force a poor soul into believing in government and business.

—Tom Robbins

Can you walk on water? You have done no better than a straw. Can you fly in the air? You have done no better than a bluebottle. Conquer your heart; then you may become somebody.

—Ansari of Herat

Even memory is not necessary for love. There is a land of the living and a land of the dead, and the bridge is love, the only survival, the only meaning.

—Thornton Wilder

○ ○ ○ ○ ○

Love is when I am concerned with your relationship with your own life, rather than with your relationship to mine. . . . There must be a commitment to each other's well-being. Most people who say they have a commitment don't; they have an attachment. Commitment means,

"I am going to stick with you and support your experience of well-being." Attachment means, "I am stuck without you."

—Stewart Emery

And someday there shall be such closeness that when one cries the other shall taste salt.

—Source unknown

It is sublime to think and say of another, I need never meet, or speak, or write to him: we need not reinforce ourselves, or send tokens of remembrance; I rely on him as on myself: if he did thus and thus, I know it was right.

—Ralph Waldo Emerson

We have often heard it said that God never closes one door unless he opens another. It is a great comfort to know we never really lose when we believe, for any defeat can be turned to good if we will absorb the lesson in it. And yet, how often we refuse to go through that door that has been opened for us. It is so much easier to stand back and wail about the closed one. There seems to be a certain amount of glorification in defeat. Sometimes a door will close for us because that particular one would have caused us more unhappiness, but it never closes for punishment. God is love—and love does not punish, nor does it have any power but to give what is right and good for us. With this knowledge we can walk with grace through those doors that open to us.

—Joyce Hifler

We have to surpass the Enlightenment notion that in the life of the species or of the individual there is a definitive changeover from darkness to light. Light is always light in darkness; that is what the unconscious is all about. Nor can the light become a current, always turned on, in ordinary prosaic language. Truth is always in poetic form; not literal but symbolic; hiding, or veiled; light in darkness. Yes, mysterious. Literalism is idolatry of words; the alternative to idolatry is mystery.

—Norman O. Brown

Compulsion is being trapped in a known psychic reality, a dead-end space. Freedom is in the unknown. If you believe there is an unknown everywhere, in your own body, in your relationships with other people, in political institutions, in the universe, then you have maximum freedom. If you can examine old beliefs and realize they are limits to be overcome and can also realize you don't have to have a belief about something you don't yet know anything about, you are free.

—John C. Lilly

One can never pay in gratitude; one can only pay "in kind" somewhere else in life.

—Anne Morrow Lindbergh

○ ○ ○ ○ ○

The whole order of things is as outrageous as any miracle which could presume to violate it.

—G.K. Chesterton

I don't paint things. I only paint the difference between things.

—Henri Matisse

The fish trap exists because of the fish. Once you've gotten the fish you can forget the trap. The rabbit snare exists because of the rabbit. Once you've gotten the rabbit, you can forget the snare. Words exist because of meaning. Once you've gotten the meaning, you can forget the words. Where can I find a man who has forgotten words so I can talk with him?

—Chuang Tzu

God offers to every mind its choice between truth and repose. Take which you please; you can never have both.

—Ralph Waldo Emerson

All the passions produce prodigies. A gambler is capable of watching and fasting almost like a saint; he has his premonitions, etc. There is a great danger of loving God as the gambler loves his game.

—Simone Weil

When a man is wrapped up in himself, he makes a pretty small package.

—John Ruskin

"What is REAL?" asked the Rabbit one day, when they were lying side by side near the nursery fender, before Nana came to tidy the room. "Does it mean having things that buzz inside you and a stick-out handle?"

"Real isn't how you are made," said the Skin Horse. "It's a thing that happens to you. When a child loves you for a long, long time, not just to play with, but REALLY loves you, then you become Real."

"Does it hurt?" asked the Rabbit.

"Sometimes," said the Skin Horse, for he was always truthful. "When you are Real you don't mind being hurt."

"Does it happen all at once, like being wound up," he asked, "or bit by bit?"

"It doesn't happen all at once," said the Skin Horse, "You become. It takes a long time. That's why it doesn't often happen to people who break easily, or have sharp edges, or who have to be carefully kept. Generally, by the time you are Real, most of your hair has been loved off, and your eyes drop out, and you get loose in the joints and very shabby. But these things don't matter at all, because once you are Real you can't be ugly, except to people who don't understand."

—Margery Williams
The Velveteen Rabbit

○ ○ ○ ○ ○

The best politics is right action.

—Mahatma Gandhi

It is only the religious mind that is a truly revolutionary mind.

—J. Krishnamurti

The penalty that good men pay for not being interested in politics is to be governed by men worse than themselves.

—Plato

Yes, I felt closer to my fellow men, too, even in my solitude. For it is not physical solitude that actually separates one from other men, not physical isolation, but spiritual isolation. It is not the desert island nor the stony wilderness that cuts you from the people you love. It is the wilderness in the mind, the desert wastes in the heart through which one wanders lost and a stranger. When one is a stranger to oneself then one is estranged from others, too. If one is out of touch with oneself, then one cannot touch others. How often in a large city, shaking hands with my friends, I have felt the wilderness stretching between us. Both of us were wandering in arid wastes, having lost the springs that nourished us—or having found them dry. Only when one is connected to one's own core is one connected to others, I am beginning to discover. And, for me, the core, the inner spring, can best be refound through solitude.

—Anne Morrow Lindbergh
Gift From The Sea

Revolutionary consciousness is to be found
Among the most ruthlessly exploited masses:
Animals, trees, water, air, grasses.

—Gary Snyder

It is simply untrue that all our institutions are evil, that all adults are unsympathetic, that all politicians are mere opportunists, that all aspects of university life are corrupt. Having discovered an illness, it's not terribly useful to prescribe death as a cure.

—George McGovern

Believe those who are seeking the truth; doubt those who find it.

—André Gide

Political life neither provides our final end nor contains the happiness we seek for ourselves or others. . . . The purpose of temporal tranquility, which well-ordered policies establish and maintain, is to give opportunities for contemplating truth.

—St. Thomas Aquinas

"The things we see," Pistorius said softly, "are the same things that are within us. There is no reality except the one contained within us. That is why so many people live such unreal lives. They take the images outside them for reality and never allow the world within to assert itself."

—Hermann Hesse
Demian

When we first experience true ordinariness, it is something very extraordinarily ordinary, so much so that we would say that mountains are not mountains anymore or streams streams anymore, because we see them as so ordinary, so precise, so "as they are." This extraordinariness derives from the experience of discovery. But eventually this superordinariness, this precision, becomes an everyday event, something we live with all the time, truly ordinary, and we are back where we started: the mountains are mountains and streams are streams. Then we can relax.

—Chögyam Trungpa
Cutting Through Spiritual Materialism

The whole earth is in jail and we're plotting this incredible jailbreak.

—Hugh Romney
aka Wavy Gravy

O O O O O

The great heresy and the only real heresy is the idea that anything is separate, distinct, and different essentially from other things. That is a wandering from natural fact and law, for nature is nothing if not coordination, cooperation, mutual helpfulness; and the rule of fundamental unity is perfectly universal: everything in the universe lives for everything else.

—G. dePurucker
Golden Precepts

If our life lacks a constant magic it is because we choose to observe our acts and lose ourselves in consideration of their imagined form instead of being impelled by their force.

—Antonin Artaud

When your ass itches, scratch it! You gotta be internal, man. . . .

—Laramie Down
Robert Coover's
The Square Shooter And The Saint

Simply to have all the necessities of life and three meals a day will not bring happiness. Happiness is hidden in the unnecessary and in those impractical things that bring delight to the inner person. . . . When we lack proper time for the simple pleasures of life, for the enjoyment of eating, drinking, playing, creating, visiting friends, and watching children at play, then we have missed the purpose of life. Not on bread alone do we live but on all these human and heart-hungry luxuries.

—Ed Hays
Pray Always

Rest does not come from sleeping but from waking.

—*A Course In Miracles*

Disillusion is the last illusion.

—Wallace Stevens

The important thing is to know how to take all things quietly.

—Michael Faraday

It is a grave misconception to regard the mystical progress as passing mostly through ecstasies and raptures. On the contrary, it passes just as much through broken hearts and bruised emotions, through painful sacrifices and melancholy renunciations.

—Paul Brunton

It costs so much to be a full human being that there are very few who have the enlightenment or the courage to pay the price. . . .

One has to abandon altogether the search for security, and reach out to the risk of living with both arms. One has to embrace the world like a lover. One has to accept pain as a condition of existence. One has to court doubt and darkness as the cost of knowing. One needs a will stubborn in conflict, but apt always to total acceptance of every consequence of living and dying.

—Morris L. West
The Shoes Of The Fisherman

A friend of mine took a Zen Buddhist monk to hear the Boston Symphony perform Beethoven's Fifth Symphony. His comment was, "Not enough silence!"

—Winthrop Sargent

The mark of your ignorance is the depth of your belief in injustice and tragedy. What the caterpillar calls the end of the world, the master calls a butterfly.

—Richard Bach
Illusions

○ ○ ○ ○ ○

I imagine one of the reasons people cling to their hates so stubbornly is because they sense, once hate is gone, they will be forced to deal with pain.

—James Baldwin

You will not grow if you sit in a beautiful flower garden, but you will grow if you are sick, if you are in pain, if you experience losses, and if you do not put your head in the sand, but take the pain and learn to accept it, not as a curse or punishment but as a gift to you with a very, very specific purpose.

—Elisabeth Kübler-Ross

Nevertheless the flowers fall with our attachment, and the weeds spring up with our aversion.

—Dogen

April is a promise that May is bound to keep.

—Hal Borland

Not that I want to be a god or hero. Just to change into a tree, grow for ages, not hurt anyone.

—Czeslaw Milosz

I tore myself away from the safe comfort of certainties through my love for truth; and truth rewarded me.

—Simone de Beauvoir
All Said And Done

I do not know which to prefer,
The beauty of inflections
Or the beauty of innuendoes,
The blackbird whistling
Or just after.

—Wallace Stevens
"Thirteen Ways Of Looking At A Blackbird"

. . . Sometimes I wonder if we were those two people nearly twenty years ago along Via Nazionale; two people who talked so politely, so urbanely, in the sunset; who chatted about everything, and nothing; two pleasant talkers, two young intellectuals out for a walk; so young, so polite, so distracted, so ready to judge each other with absent kindliness, so ready to say goodbye forever, in that sunset, on that street corner.

—Natalia Ginzburg

When I have to cut tapes, in the places where the speaker sometimes pauses for a moment—or sighs, or takes a breath, or there is absolute silence—I don't throw that away, I collect it. I splice it together and play back the tape when I'm at home in the evening.

—Heinrich Böll

Until I feared I would lose it, I never loved to read. One does not love breathing.

—Harper Lee
To Kill A Mockingbird

Interviewer: Some people say they can't understand your writing even after they read it two or three times. What approach would you suggest for them?

William Faulkner: Read it four times.
—*William Faulkner: Three Decades Of Criticism*
F.J. Hoffman and O.W. Vickery, eds.

We don't know who discovered water, but we're certain it wasn't a fish.

—John Culkin

The complexities of life situations are really not as complicated as we tend to experience them.
—Chögyam Trungpa

"Yes, Siddhartha," he said. "Is this what you mean? That the river is everywhere at the same time, at the source and at the mouth, at the waterfalls, at the ferry, at the current, in the ocean and in the mountains, everywhere, and that the present only exists for it, not the shadow of the past, nor the shadow of the future?"

"That it is," said Siddhartha, "and when I learned that, I reviewed my life and it was also a river, and Siddhartha the boy, Siddhartha the mature man, and Siddhartha the old man were only separated by shadows, not through reality. Siddhartha's previous lives were also not in the past, and his death and his return to Brahma are not in the future. Nothing was, nothing will be, everything has reality and presence."

—Hermann Hesse
Siddhartha

As long as we have some definite idea about or some hope in the future, we cannot really be serious with the moment that exists right now.
—Suzuki Roshi
Zen Mind, Beginner's Mind

Live your questions now, and perhaps even without knowing it, you will live along some distant day into your answers.

—Rainer Maria Rilke

Somebody was saying to Picasso that he ought to make pictures of things the way they are—

objective pictures. He mumbled he wasn't quite sure what that would be. The person who was bullying him produced a photograph of his wife from his wallet and said, "There, you see, that is a picture of how she really is." Picasso looked at it and said, "She is rather small, isn't she? And flat?"

—Gregory Bateson

Art is the lie that reveals truth.

—Pablo Picasso

A wise man is never less alone than when he is alone.

—Jonathan Swift

The purpose of discipline is to promote freedom. But freedom leads to infinity and infinity is terrifying.

—Henry Miller

We are the living links in a life force that moves and plays through and around us, binding the deepest soils with the farthest stars.

—Alan Chadwick

Civilized man has exchanged some part of his chances of happiness for a measure of security.

—Sigmund Freud

What is life? It is the flash of a firefly in the night. It is the breath of a buffalo in the wintertime. It is the little shadow which runs across the grass and loses itself in the sunset.

—Crowfoot

I am malicious because I am miserable; if any being felt emotions of benevolence toward me,

I should return them, a hundred and a hundred fold.

—Frankenstein monster
Mary Shelley's *Frankenstein*

○ ○ ○ ○ ○

Though no two centuries are very much like each other, some hours perhaps are; moments are; critical moments nearly always are. Emotions are the same. We are the same. The man, not the day, is the lasting phenomenon.

—Eudora Welty

To know someone here or there with whom you feel there is understanding in spite of differences or thoughts expressed—that can make of this earth a garden.

—Johann Wolfgang von Goethe

If I am transparent enough to myself, then I can become less afraid of those hidden selves that my transparency may reveal to others. If I reveal myself without worrying about how others will respond, then some will care, though others may not. But who can love me, if no one knows me? I must risk it, or live alone. It is enough that I must die alone. I am determined to let down, whatever the risks, if it means that I may have whatever is there for me.

—Sheldon Kopp
If You Meet The Buddha On The Road, Kill Him

Gandhi said your power becomes invincible when you have reduced yourself to zero—which means, when you don't want anything, when you have no more fear looking in the eyes of death, when you're right here. Then your statement has the power of the universe behind it. It's coming from a root place of truth, because there's nothing in it for you. You don't want anything.

To me, that is the power of a Christ, or just one clear person who isn't vulnerable. I don't underestimate the power of the human heart. When I look at the human heart, that link, that doorway, I see an institution that makes the Pentagon look like kids' toys.

—Ram Dass

Everybody's fame is in his own universe. Everybody is the center of his own universe. When you have a million people, you turn up the volume on your own ego and you get to see it bigger, or you can. You can ignore it and think that it's all real and that you are the universe, but otherwise if you're a bit open and have some space around your head, you can actually make use of that situation to examine your own passion, your own attachment, your own egocentricity. And because it's stuck right in front of your nose like naked lunch you may get a little more insight into it and actually be in an advantageous position to make your own egocentricity more transparent.

—Allen Ginsberg

Respect for the vulnerability of human beings is a necessary part of telling the truth, because no truth will be wrested from a callous vision or callous handling.

—Anaïs Nin

No matter how many communes anybody invents, the family always creeps back.

—Margaret Mead

The union of the family lies in love; and love is the only reconciliation of authority and liberty.

—Robert H. Benson

There is nothing outside you. That is what you must ultimately learn.

—*A Course In Miracles*

○ ○ ○ ○ ○

Great mother of big apples it is a pretty world.

—Kenneth Patchen

There is really no such creature as a single individual; he has no more life of his own than a cast-off cell marooned from the surface of your skin.

—Lewis Thomas

I argued that physical discomfort is important only when the mood is wrong. Then you fasten on to whatever thing is uncomfortable and call that the cause. But if the mood is right, then physical discomfort doesn't mean much.

—Robert M. Pirsig
Zen And The Art Of Motorcycle Maintenance

All of us . . . have been formed by experiences that still inhabit us. Memory is not only a trip but also a structure. Recollections are not only stories retold but also aspects of present feeling. Our hopes at any given moment are fashioned by our previous disappointment. Our need to share pain is as strong as our quest for pleasure. Every pain that is not purely physical is also retrospective. Our need to make sense of our lives has continually to take account of all this.

—John Berger

If you've not been fed, be bread.

—Jelaluddin Rumi

There is not one big cosmic meaning for all, there is only the meaning we each give to our life. . . . To seek a total unity is wrong. To give as much meaning to one's life as possible is right to me.

—Anaïs Nin

I have had more trouble with myself than with any man I have ever met.

—Dwight Moody

There is no way to peace. Peace is the way.

—A.J. Muste

I shall tell you a great secret, my friend. Do not wait for the last judgement. It takes place every day.

—Albert Camus
The Fall

You know you can never find out what's happening from the company bulletin or the adult press. You know that. The king's messengers are always telling you what they want you to know, for their own benefit. The evolutionary message, what's really happening, has always come from outcasts.

—Timothy Leary

Everything we come across is to the point.

—John Cage

The most instructive experiences are those of everyday life.

—Friedrich Nietzsche

The sin against the Holy Spirit is the sin against new life, against self-emergence, against the Holy fecund innerness of each person. It can be committed quite as easily against oneself as against another.

—M.C. Richards

You might as well fall flat on your face as lean over too far backward.

—James Thurber

At times, although one is perfectly in the right, one's legs tremble; at other times, although one is completely in the wrong, birds sing in one's soul.

—V.V. Rozinov

Things don't change, but by and by our wishes change.

—Marcel Proust

○ ○ ○ ○ ○

The winds of grace blow all the time. All we need to do is set our sails.

—Ramakrishna

The difficulty is to learn to perceive with your whole body, not with just your eyes and reason.

The world becomes a stream of tremendously rapid, unique events. So you must trim your body to make it a good receptor. The body is an awareness; and it must be treated impeccably.

—Carlos Castaneda

There is an artistry of experience which precedes the artistry of creation.

—Matthew Lipman

True light that makes true vision possible is not the light the body's eyes behold. It is a state of mind that has been so unified that darkness cannot be perceived.

—*A Course In Miracles*

No one worth possessing can be quite possessed.

—Sara Teasdale

It always comes back to the same necessity: go deep enough and there is a bedrock of truth, however hard.

—May Sarton

Gossip isn't scandal and it isn't malicious. It's chatter about the human race by lovers of the same.

—Phyllis McGinley

No; we have been as usual asking the wrong question. It does not matter a hoot what the mockingbird on the chimney is singing. . . . The real and proper question is: why is it beautiful?

—Annie Dillard
Pilgrim at Tinker Creek

The difference between a moral man and a man of honor is that the latter regrets a discreditable act, even when it has worked and he has not been caught.

—Henry Mencken

Everything is funny as long as it's happening to somebody else.

—Will Rogers

If we could read the secret history of those we would like to punish, we would find in each life enough grief and suffering to make us stop wishing anything more on them.

—Source unknown

Neither the word "free" nor any corresponding term occurs in the root language, in the primal concept; there was never anything for the Indian to free himself from. His spirit was not seeking truth but holding on to truth. And his was the mind nourished by choice. Whatever he needed to know was sooner or later revealed to him. And that which he desired to know—the best way to achieve his maximum spiritual potential—was the only mystery he chose to investigate.

—Ruth Beebe Hill
Hanta Yo

Things often happen like that. Many people who accepted Stalin—that is, who accepted the unacceptable—didn't do so out of self-interest, but simply because at that moment they had other things to do which seemed essential and which distracted them from the atrocity. It's a rather poignant historical phenomenon, and one which is difficult to ignore. There is no

abstract ethical system, any more than there is an absolute hierarchy of choices. There are only individual situations and people to be faced, and all we can do is to deal with them expeditiously.

I believe that dignity changes history in the long run. That's the reason I have often spoken of brotherhood. I'm well aware that expression has two meanings, too. There's Christian brotherhood which comes directly from the notion of a saintly communion that's not so bad. And there was a revolutionary brotherhood.

But don't these two kinds of brotherhood have something in common? In both cases the other is seen as more important than oneself. It's a very old idea. You ask if it could change history. I wonder if it hasn't already changed it profoundly. We are evolving from the farthest reaches of time, and I don't know if what impresses me most is the enormity of what is behind us or the enormity of what lies ahead.

— André Malraux

You've got to have something to eat and a little love in your life before you can hold still for any damn body's sermon on how to behave.

— Billie Holiday

Since when was genius respectable?

— Elizabeth Barrett Browning

What I love about sex is that it is never completed. You think it is finished and you realize you never get there. I think of a prism.

— Anica Vesel Mander

Freedom means choosing your burden.

— Hephzibah Menuhin

The pain of love is the pain of being alive. It's a perpetual wound.

— Maureen Duffy

The Lord God is subtle, but malicious He is not.

— Albert Einstein

○ ○ ○ ○ ○

Just because the spiritual master lets you call him by his first name doesn't mean he isn't dangerous.

— Source unknown

I wasn't kissing her, I was whispering in her mouth.

— Chico Marx

If you tell the truth, you have infinite power supporting you; but if not, you have infinite power against you.

— Charles Gordon

An honorable human relationship—that is, one in which two people have the right to use the word "love"—is a process, delicate, violent, often terrifying to both persons involved, a process of refining the truths they can tell each other. It is important to do this because it breaks down human self-delusion and isolation. It is important to do this because in so doing we do justice to our own complexity. It is important to do this because we can count on so few people to go that hard way with us.

—Adrienne Rich

A Taoist master was sitting naked in his mountain cabin, meditating. A group of Confucianists entered the door of his hut, having hiked up the mountain intending to lecture him on the rules of proper conduct. When they saw the sage sitting naked before them, they were shocked, and asked, "What are you doing, sitting in your hut without any pants on?" The sage replied, "This entire universe is my hut. This little hut is my pants. What are you fellows doing inside my pants?"

—James N. Powell

Ideologies separate us. Dreams and anguish bring us together.

—Eugene Ionesco

When childhood dies, its corpses are called adults.

—Brian Aldiss

If one should be shown odd fragments arranged on a silver tray and be told, "That is a splinter from the True Cross, and that is a nail paring dropped by Barabbas, and that is a bit of lint from under the bed where Pilate's wife dreamed her dream," the very ordinariness of the things would recommend them. Every spirit passing through the world fingers the tangible and mars the mutable, and finally has come to look and not to buy. So shoes are worn and hassocks are sat upon and finally everything is left where it was and the spirit passes on, just as the wind in the orchard picks up the leaves from the ground as if there were no other pleasure in the world but brown leaves, as if it would deck, clothe, flesh itself in flourishes of dusty brown apple leaves, and then drops them all in a heap at the side of the house and goes on.

—Marilynne Robinson
Housekeeping

Conscious faith is freedom. Emotional faith is slavery. Mechanical faith is foolishness.

—G.I. Gurdjieff

The most fundamental of divisions is that between the intellect, which can only do its work by saying continually, "Thou fool," and the religious genius which makes all equal.

—William Butler Yeats

At the day's end
all our footsteps are added up
to see how near.

—W.S. Merwin
"Last People"

○ ○ ○ ○ ○

Life is short and it hurts. Love is the only drug that works.

—John Coit

God created man, and finding him not sufficiently alone, gave him a female companion so that he might feel his solitude more acutely.

—Paul Valéry

I like trees because they seem more resigned to the way they have to live than other things do.

—Willa Cather

Men are always sincere. They change sincerities, that's all.

—Tristan Bernard

Childhood is not only the childhood we really had but also the impressions we formed of it in our adolescence and maturity. That is why childhood seems so long. Probably every period of life is multiplied by our reflections upon it in the next. The shortest is old age because we shall never be able to think back on it.

—Cesare Pavese

What can a flame remember? If it remembers a little less than is necessary, it goes out; if it remembers a little more than is necessary, it goes out. If only it could teach us, while it burns, to remember correctly.

—George Seferis

To me, old age is always fifteen years older than I am.

—Bernard M. Baruch
upon observing his eighty-fifth birthday

The tragedy of old age is not that one is old, but that one is young.

—Oscar Wilde

Our mind is capable of passing beyond the dividing line we have drawn for it. Beyond the pairs of opposites of which the world consists, other, new insights begin.

—Hermann Hesse

One of the two things that people who have lasted for a hundred years always say: either that they have drunk whiskey and smoked all their lives, or that neither tobacco nor spirits ever made the faintest appeal to them.

—Edward Verrall Lucas

In the difficult are the friendly forces, the hands that work on us.

—Rainer Maria Rilke

Make sure to send a lazy man for the Angel of Death.

—Yiddish proverb

The grand show is eternal. It is always sunrise somewhere; the dew is never all dried at once; a shower is forever falling; vapor is ever rising. Eternal sunrise, eternal dawn and gloaming, on sea and continents and islands, each in its turn, as the round earth rolls.

—John Muir

○ ○ ○ ○ ○

When a dog runs at you, whistle for him.

—Henry David Thoreau

We are what we imagine. Our very existence consists in our imagination of ourselves. The greatest tragedy that can befall us is to go unimagined.

—N. Scott Mornaday

Close your hand—do you feel an absence or a presence?

—Brenda Hefty

Most lives are a flight from selfhood. Most prefer the truths of the stable. You stick your head into the stanchions and munch contentedly until you die. Others use you for their purposes. Not once do you look outside the stable to lift your head and be your own creature.

—Frank Herbert
Children Of Dune

War is sex perverted.

—Norman O. Brown

And I remembered *The Fourteenth Book Of Bokonon*, which I had read in its entirety the night before. *The Fourteenth Book* is entitled, "What Can A Thoughtful Man Hope For Mankind On Earth, Given The Experience Of The Past Million Years?" It doesn't take long to read *The Fourteenth Book*. It consists of one word and a period.

This is it.

"Nothing."

—Kurt Vonnegut, Jr.
Cat's Cradle

. . . Here we are in Science Fiction History, in the age of Hydrogen Bomb Apocalypse, the very Kali Yuga wherein man's stupidity so over-whelms the planet that ecological catastrophe begins to rehearse old tribe tales of Karmic retribution, Fire and Flood and Armageddon impending.

—Allen Ginsberg

Peace is not an absence of war, it is a virtue, a state of mind, a disposition for benevolence, confidence, justice.

—Baruch Spinoza

Remember that you came to bring the peace of God into the world.

—*A Course In Miracles*

Thinking about interior peace destroys interior peace. The patient who constantly feels his pulse is not getting any better.

—Hubert van Zeller

There is no evil in the universe which is not the result of ignorance, and which would not, if we were ready and willing to learn its lesson, lead us to a higher wisdom, and then vanish away.

—James Allan

The atomic bomb is the real Buddha of the West, a perfect detached sovereign apparatus. Unmoving, it rests in its silo, purest actuality and purest potentiality. It is the embodiment of cosmic energies and the human share in these, the highest accomplishment of the human race, and its destroyer; the triumph of technical rationality, and its dissolution into paranoia. Its repose and its irony are endless. It is the same to the bomb how it fulfills its mission, whether in silent waiting or as a cloud of fire. For it, the change of conditioned states does not count.

As with a Buddha, all there is to say is said by its mere existence. It is not a bit more evil than reality, and not a hair more destructive than we are. It is already completely incarnate, while we in comparison are still divided. In the face of such an instrument, great listening is called for. Rather than strategic considerations, the bomb requires from us neither struggle nor resignation, but experience of ourselves. We are it.

—Peter Slutterton

○ ○ ○ ○ ○

Man with wooden leg escapes prison. He's caught. They take his wooden leg away from him. Each day he must cross a large hill and swim a wide river to get to the field where he must work all day on one leg. This goes on for a year. At the Christmas party they give him back his leg. Now he doesn't want it. His escape is all planned. It requires only one leg.

—James Tate

The curious paradox is that when I accept myself just as I am, then I can change.

—Carl Rogers

Whereas I formerly believed it to be my bounden duty to call other persons to order, I now admit that I need calling to order myself.

—Carl Jung

There is a very profound truth in the Greek sophisms proving that it is impossible to learn. We understand little and badly. We need to be taught by those who understand more and better than ourselves. For example, by Christ. But since we do not understand anything, we do not understand them either. How could we know that they are right? How could we pay them the proper amount of attention, to begin with, which is necessary before they can begin to teach us? That is why miracles are needed.

—Simone Weil

Every illusion carries pain and suffering in the dark folds of the heavy garments in which it hides its nothingness.

—A Course In Miracles

In the service of God, you can learn three things from a child, and seven from a thief. From a child you can learn: (1) always to be happy; (2) never to sit idle; and (3) to cry for everything one wants. From a thief you should learn: (1) to work at night; (2) if one cannot gain what one wants in one night to try again the next night; (3) to love one's co-workers just as thieves love each other; (4) to be willing to risk one's life even for a little thing; (5) not to attach too much value to things even though one has risked one's life for them—just as a thief will resell a stolen article for a fraction of its real value; (6) to withstand all kinds of beatings and tortures but to remain what you are; and (7) to believe that your work is worthwhile and not be willing to change it.

—Dov Baer, the Mazid of Mezeritch
quoted in The Wisdom Of The Jewish Mystics

God speaks to all individuals through what happens to them moment by moment.

—Jean Pierre de Caussade

You can hold back from the suffering of the world, you have free permission to do so, and it is in accordance with your nature, but perhaps this very holding back is the one suffering you could have avoided.

—Franz Kafka

Although the world is very full of suffering, it is also full of the overcoming of it.

—Helen Keller

While others talked about what they would do if they heard that they had to die within that very hour, St. Charles Borromaeus said he would continue his game of chess. For he had begun it only in honor of God, and he could wish for nothing better than to be called away in the midst of an action undertaken in the honor of God.

—William Faber

○ ○ ○ ○ ○

The day was counting up its birds and never got the answer right.

—Source unknown

If a man gives way to all his desires, or panders to them, there will be no inner struggle in him, no friction, no fire. But if, for the sake of attaining a definite aim, he struggles with desires that hinder him, he will then create a fire which will gradually transform his inner world into a single whole.

—P.D. Ouspensky
In Search Of The Miraculous

Interviewer: How much rewriting do you do?

Hemingway: It depends. I rewrote the ending of *A Farewell to Arms*, the last page of it, thirty-nine times before I was satisfied.

Interviewer: Was there some technical problem there? What was it that had stumped you?

Hemingway: Getting the words right.

—*Paris Review*

It is one of the great troubles of life that we cannot have any unmixed emotions. There is always something in our enemy that we like, and something in our sweetheart that we dislike.

—William Butler Yeats

All men's misfortunes spring from their hatred of being alone.

—Jean de La Bruyère

It is never any good dwelling on goodbyes. It is not the being together that it prolongs, it is the parting.

—Elizabeth Bibesco

Beauty is a terrible and awful thing! It is terrible because it has not been fathomed and never can be fathomed, for God sets us nothing but riddles. . . . The devil only knows what to make of it! What to the mind is shameful is beauty and nothing else to the heart. Is there beauty in Sodom? Believe me, that for the immense mass of mankind, beauty is found in Sodom. Did you know that secret? The awful thing is that beauty is mysterious as well as terrible. God and the devil are fighting there and the battle-

102

field is the heart of man. But a man always talks of his own ache.

—Fyodor Dostoyevsky
The Brothers Karamazov

By your stumbling, the world is perfected.

—Sri Aurobindo

○ ○ ○ ○ ○

My life is my message.

—Mahatma Gandhi

The highest possible stage in moral culture is when we recognize that we ought to control our thoughts.

—Charles Darwin

The end move in politics is always to pick up a gun.

—R. Buckminster Fuller

I respect the man who knows distinctly what he wishes. The greater part of all the mischief in the world arises from the fact that men do not sufficiently understand their own aims. They have undertaken to build a tower, and spend no more labor on the foundation than would be necessary to erect a hut.

—Johann Wolfgang von Goethe

When you exhale you must exhale all of Mt. Baldy [a Zen center]. When you inhale you must inhale all of this world. If you think about combining the two, that is misleading. Instead you have to realize that there are two separate lives. It is wrong to set up the self and try to adjust the outside world to it. Instead, give the self to both worlds which are real and necessary. At one time, you must leave your girlfriend and live alone. At the other time you must be with her. To be alone and to be together, these can be freely repeated. That is real life. To go to the toilet is done by the self and to eat food is also done by the self. Americans think, "Which is the real self, to go to the toilet or to eat?" You are doing both.

—Suzuki Roshi

We shall not cease from exploration and the end of all our exploring will be to arrive where we started and know the place for the first time.

—T.S. Eliot

If you're going to be an artist, all life is your subject. And all your experience is part of your art. A youngster told me recently that he was going to give himself a year to see if he has talent. A year! It takes a lifetime to see if you have it. Painting is a total engagement.

—Ben Shahn

We are what we pretend to be, so we must be careful about what we pretend to be.

—Kurt Vonnegut, Jr.

One is not rich by what one owns, but more by what one is able to do without with dignity.

—Immanuel Kant

I love her and she loves me and together we hate each other with a wild hatred born of love.

—Edvard Munch

People need a little loving and, God, sometimes it's sad all the shit they have to go through to find some.

—Richard Brautigan

Were art to redeem man, it could do so only by saving him from the seriousness of life and restoring to him an unexpected boyishness.

—José Ortega y Gasset

The solution of the problem of life is seen in the vanishing of the problem. Is not this the reason why those who have found after a long period of doubt that the sense of life became clear have then been unable to say what constituted that sense?

—Ludwig Wittgenstein

The fabled musk deer searches the world over for the source of the scent which comes from itself.

—Ramakrishna

Sometimes you win, sometimes you lose, sometimes you get rained out.

—Satchel Paige

There is neither creation nor destruction, neither destiny nor free will, neither path nor achievement; this is the final truth.

—Ramana Maharshi

He rather likes people who fight Him. Fighting God, fighting Judaism, means that you are active, not passive, within it. If I don't care about it, then I have no questions, and if I have no questions, then I have no problems. If I do care about it, then I'll be questioning it, and I'll definitely have more problems with it because the questions lead to problems, not answers. In a certain way the difference between a saint and someone who is surely not a saint is not that the saint has no problems, but that he has more, and more elaborate, problems. It is an incessant struggle.

—Adin Steinsaltz

Every gun that is made, every warship launched, every rocket fired signifies, in the final sense, a theft from those who hunger and are not fed, those who are cold and are not clothed.

This world in arms is not spending money alone. It is spending the sweat of its laborers, the genius of its scientists, the hopes of its children. The cost of one modern heavy bomber is this: a modern brick school in more than thirty cities. It is two electric power plants, each serving a town of 60,000. It is two fine, fully equipped hospitals. It is some fifty miles of concrete highway. We pay for a single destroyer with new homes that could have housed more than 8,000 people.

This, I repeat, is the best way of life to be found on the road the world has been taking.

This is not a way of life at all, in any true sense. Under the cloud of threatening war, it is humanity hanging from a cross of iron.

—President Dwight D. Eisenhower
(April 16, 1953)

When one is pretending the entire body revolts.
—Anaïs Nin

Whether one walks, rides a camel, flies, or dives deep into the sea, it is for the sole purpose of crossing a frontier beyond which man ceases to feel himself the master, sure of his techniques, upheld by his inheritance, backed by the crowd. The more powerless he is, the more his spirit permeates his being. The horizon of the world and the horizon of thought coincide within him. Then the water, the rocks, and the sand become vital nourishment, and perhaps a poem.
—Philippe Diole

A happy childhood can't be cured. Mine'll hang around my neck like a rainbow, that's all, instead of a noose.
—Hortense Calisher

Who sees variety and not the unity wanders on from death to death.
—*The Upanishads*

Even as radio waves are picked up wherever a set is tuned in to their wavelength, so the thoughts which each of us think each moment of the day go forth into the world to influence for good or bad each other human mind.
—Christmas Humphreys

Nothing can fill the gap when we are away from those we love, and it would be wrong to try and find anything. We must simply hold out and win through. That sounds very hard at first, but at the same time it is a great consolation, since leaving the gap unfilled preserves the bonds between us. It is nonsense to say that God fills the gap; he does not fill it, but keeps it empty so that our communion with one another may be kept alive, even at the cost of pain.
—Dietrich Bonhoffer

It takes a long time to become young.
—Pablo Picasso

○ ○ ○ ○ ○

The pure in heart will avoid the struggles, detour the tar pits, blind their eyes to the sirens. The problem is that in avoiding the paths that contain the tar, you may never reach any destination; in avoiding temptation, you remain pure, but irrelevant. Life is tar pits and sirens.
—Donald A. Norman

The problem is not that there are problems. The problem is expecting otherwise and thinking that having problems is a problem.

—Theodore Rubin

We awake suddenly in the middle of the night, and perceive infinite time exploding beyond us; we stare through the dark room at a universe that has existed for trillions of years before we were conceived. So macabre, so astonishing, so unlikely! In the consequence of all this our life seems a worthless thing, a trick. But who is there to trick?

—Richard Grossinger
Embryogenesis

In the shadow of his hand hath he hid me.

—*Isaiah 49:2*

When I was a child . . . I would think it must be marvelous to issue those proclamations of experience—"It was at least ten years ago" or "I hadn't seen him for twenty years." But chronological prestige is tenacious: once attained, it can't be shed; it increases moment by moment, day by day, pressing its honors on you until you are lavishly, overly endowed with them. Until you literally sink under them.

—Shirley Hazzard
The Bay Of Noon

A child is the root of the heart.

—Carolina María de Jesús

First we were nothing. Now we are something. After a little we shall be nothing again. The interval, while we are something, seems immensely important; we agonize over it terri-

bly. Even if some wise person soothes us by setting our toothache in a perspective of light-years, galaxies, spiral nebulae, the toothache continues to hurt as though it has not heard. Toothaches can sometimes be dealt with by dentists, but never by philosophers. Life is very short, a brief instant of light; but every instant of it may contain all eternity.

—Howard Nemerov
Journal Of The Fictive Life

Even without wars, life is dangerous.

—Anne Sexton

For you, the world is weird because if you're not bored with it you're at odds with it. For me the world is weird because it is stupendous, awesome, mysterious, unfathomable; my interest has been to convince you that you must assume responsibility for being here, in this marvelous world, in this marvelous desert, in this marvelous time. I wanted to convince you that you must learn to make every act count, since you are going to be here for only a short while, in fact, too short for witnessing all the marvels of it.

—don Juan
Carlos Castaneda's *Journey To Ixtlan*

You cannot truly listen to anyone and do anything else at the same time.

—M. Scott Peck

I've learned that next to the atomic bomb, the greatest danger is defeatism, despair, and inadequate awareness of what human beings possess. I feel that any problem that can be defined is capable of being resolved. Out of this

has come my conviction that no man knows enough to be a pessimist.

—Norman Cousins

What keeps our faith cheerful is the extreme persistence of gentleness and humor. Gentleness is everywhere in daily life, a sign that faith rules through ordinary things: through cooking and small talk, through storytelling, making love, fishing, tending animals and sweet corn and flowers, through sports, music, and books, raising kids—all the places where the gravy soaks in and grace shines through. Even in a time of elephantine vanity and greed, one never has to look far to see the campfires of gentle people. Lacking any other purpose in life, it would be good enough to live for their sake.

—Garrison Keillor

Those who wish to sing always find a song.

—Swedish proverb

○ ○ ○ ○ ○

As far as the writing itself is concerned it takes next to no time at all. Much too much is written every day of our lives. We are overwhelmed by it. But when at times we see through the welter of evasive or interested patter, when by chance we penetrate to some moving detail of a life, there is always time to bang out a few pages. The thing isn't to find the time for it—we waste hours every day doing absolutely nothing at all —the difficulty is to catch the evasive life of the thing, to phrase the words in such a way that stereotype will yield a moment of insight.

This is where the difficulty lies. We are lucky when that underground current can be tapped and the secret spring of all our lives will send up its pure water. It seldom happens. A thousand trivialities push themselves to the front, our lying habits of everyday speech and thought are foremost, telling us that *that* is what "they" want to hear. Tell them something else.

—William Carlos Williams

The man with the clear head is the man who . . . looks life in the face, realizes that everything in it is problematic, and feels himself lost. And this is the simple truth: that to live is to feel oneself lost. He who accepts it has already begun to find himself, to be on firm ground.

—José Ortega y Gasset
The Revolt Of The Masses

I have learned silence from the talkative, toleration from the intolerant, and kindness from the unkind; yet strange, I am ungrateful to these teachers.

—Kahlil Gibran

If you stop to be kind you must swerve often from your path.

—Mary Webb

What is laid down, ordered, factual is never enough to embrace the whole truth: life always spills over the rim of every cup.

—Boris Pasternak

I am reminded of the story about "Bird's Nest Roshi." He was a teacher who lived in the T'ang period and did *zazen* (meditation) in a tree. The governor of his province, Po Chu-i, heard about

Bird's Nest Roshi and went to see him. This Po Chu-i was no ordinary politician. He was one of China's greatest poets, well-known for his expression of Zen Buddhism.

Po Chu-i found Bird's Nest Roshi sitting in his trees, doing *zazen*. He called to him, saying, "Oh, Bird's Nest, you look very insecure up there. Tell me, what is it that all the buddhas taught?" Bird's Nest Roshi replied by quoting from the *Dhammapada*:

> Always do good;
> Never do evil;
> Keep your mind pure—
> Thus all the buddhas taught.

So Po Chu-i said, "Always do good; never do evil; keep your mind pure—I knew that when I was three years old."

"Yes," said Bird's Nest Roshi, "a three-year-old child may know it, but even an eighty-year-old man cannot put it into practice."
> —Robert Aitken
> · *Taking The Path Of Zen*

I am not a *complete* vegetarian. I eat only animals that have died in their sleep.
> —George Carlin

I certainly wasn't happy. Happiness has to do with reason, and only reason earns it. What I was given was the thing you can't earn, and can't keep, and often don't even recognize at the time; I mean joy.
> —Ursula K. LeGuin

Charity. To love human beings insofar as they are nothing. That is, to love them as God does.
> —Simone Weil

Love until it hurts.
> —Mother Theresa

○ ○ ○ ○ ○

The disciples were full of questions about God.

Said the master, "God is the Unknown and the Unknowable. Every statement about him, every answer to your questions, is a distortion of the truth."

The disciples were bewildered. "Then why do you speak about him at all?"

"Why does the bird sing?" said the master.
> —Anthony de Mello
> *The Song Of The Bird*

Oh bless the continuous stutter
of the Word being made into flesh.
> —Leonard Cohen

There isn't any secret formula or method. You learn love by loving—by paying attention and doing what one thereby discovers has to be done.
> —Aldous Huxley

Adam was but human—this explains it all. He did not want the apple for the apple's sake; he wanted it only because it was forbidden. The

mistake was in not forbidding the serpent—
then he would have eaten the serpent.

—Mark Twain

God instructs the heart not by ideas, but by
pains and contradictions.

—Jean Pierre de Caussade

Anything that is given can be at once taken
away. We have to learn never to expect anything, and when it comes it's no more than a
gift on loan.

—John McGahern
The Leavetaking

Be kind; everyone you meet is fighting a hard
battle.

—John Watson

You climb up through the little grades and then
get to the top and everybody cheers; with the
sweat in your eyebrows you can't see very well
and the noise swirls around you and lifts you up,
and then you're out, not forgotten at first, just
out, and it feels good and cool and free. You're
out, and sort of melt, and keep lifting, until you
become like to these kids just one more piece
of the sky of adults that hangs over them in the
town, a piece that for some queer reason has
clouded and visited them.

—John Updike
Rabbit Run

Yet no matter how deeply I go down into myself
my God is dark, and like a webbing made of a
hundred roots, that drink in silence.

—Rainer Maria Rilke

"Lady, a man is divided into two parts, body
and spirit. . . . A body and a spirit," he
repeated. "The body, lady, is like a house, it
don't go anywhere; but the spirit, lady, is like
an automobile: always on the move, always. . . ."

—Flannery O'Connor
A Good Man Is Hard To Find

The wind said
You know I'm
the result of
forces beyond my control

—A.R. Ammons
The Wide Land

It had done me good to be somewhat parched
by the heat and drenched by the rain of life.

—Henry Wadsworth Longfellow

If you were healed of a dreadful wound, you did
not want to keep the bandage.

—Ursula Reilly Curtiss
The Wasp

One has not understood until one has forgotten it.

—Suzuki Daisetz

After an hour or so in the woods looking for
mushrooms, Dad said, "Well, we can always go
and buy some real ones."

—John Cage

We talk too much; we should talk less and draw more.

—Johann Wolfgang von Goethe

You cannot explain me with "isms." They are very bad for an artist. What one must believe in is color.

—Marc Chagall

It is not the events of today that happened to you that matter (such as that you lost something or something went wrong or someone forgot you or spoke to you harshly, etc.), but how you reacted to it all—that is, what states of yourself you were in—for it is here that your real life lies and if our inner states were right nothing in the nature of external states could overcome us. Try therefore to distinguish, as an exercise in living more consciously, between inner states and outer events, and try to meet any outer event, after noticing its nature, with the right inner attitude —that is, with the right state. And if you cannot, think afterward about it—first try to define the nature of the event and notice if this kind of event often comes to you and try to see it more clearly in terms such as "This is called being late" or "This is called losing things" or "This is called receiving bad news" or "This is called unpleasant surprises" or "This is called hard work" or "This is called being ill." Begin in this very simple way and you will soon see how different personal events, and so how in this respect one's outer life, are changing all the time, and what you could not do at one moment, you can at another.

—Maurice Nicoll
Psychological Commentaries

All information is imperfect.

—Jacob Bronowski

Events are only the external form of what happens. Form carries with it no particular content. Because I once enjoyed myself during a Super Bowl, I have concluded that watching Super Bowls causes enjoyment. Or I went to several cocktail parties and did not enjoy myself and have concluded that cocktail parties cause boredom. Anticipation is always the exercise of such illogical connections. Otherwise I would feel no urge to picture the form of future events, realizing that content, not form, is the determiner of happiness, and content is always within me.

—Hugh Prather
There Is A Place Where You Are Not Alone

The only abnormality is the incapacity to love.

—Anaïs Nin

Perfectly indifferent I am!
No joy no gratefulness
Yet nothing to grieve over the absence of
    gratefulness.

—Saichi

Anxiety is the gap between the now and the later.

—Fritz Perls

What is death, I ask: what is life, you ask.

—Anne Sexton

Abandon all hope, abandon any kind of location. It is just a wonderful experience to realize that you are actually lost, just swimming. We do not know, here with this beautiful stone

Buddha, with each other in this room, where this is. Do you know where this is, where we are? If you think you know, that is not right.

—Baker Roshi

Nobody on the outside, no, not even God Himself, knows what a man suffers on the inside. There's no language to convey it. It's beyond all human comprehension. It's so vast, so wide, so deep that even the angels with all their powers of understanding and all their powers of locomotion could never explore the whole of it. No, when a friend makes a call on you you've got to obey. You have to do for him what God Himself wouldn't do. It's a law. Otherwise you'd fall apart, you'd bark in the night like a dog.

—Henry Miller
The Air-Conditioned Nightmare

○ ○ ○ ○ ○

All happy families resemble one another; every unhappy family is unhappy in its own way.

—Leo Tolstoy

Nothing has a stronger influence psychologically on their environment, and especially on their children, than the unlived life of the parents.

—Carl Jung

A little boy of five runs to his mother holding a big fat worm in his hand and says, "Mummy, look what a big fat worm I have got." She says, "You are filthy—go away and clean yourself immediately."

—R.D. Laing

What the mother sings to the cradle goes all the way down to the coffin.

—Henry Ward Beecher

We delude ourselves that we want to implant "honesty" in our children; what we really want is to imbue them with our particular kind of dishonesty, with our culture's dishonesty, our class's dishonesty, our cult's dishonesty.

—Sidney Harris

The greatest enemy of any one of our truths may be the rest of our truths.

—William James

The years come to my door and knock and walk away sighing.

—Richard Tillinghast

During the first period of a man's life the greatest danger is not to take the risk. When once the risk has been taken, then the greatest danger is to risk too much. By not risking at first one turns aside and serves trivialities; in the second case, by risking too much, one turns aside to the fantastic and perhaps to presumption.

—Sören Kierkegaard

I'm looking for the face I had before the world was made.

—William Butler Yeats

In every man there lies hidden a child between five and eight years old, the age at which naivete comes to an end. It is this child whom one must detect in that intimidating man with his long beard, bristling eyebrows, heavy mustache, and weighty look—a captain. Even he conceals, and not at all deep down, the youngster, the booby, the little rascal, out of whom age has made this powerful monster.

—Paul Valéry

Time is not a road—it is a room.

—John Fowles

This is my father, Mrs. Baines. Try what you can with him! He won't listen to me, because he remembers what a fool I was when I was a baby.

—George Bernard Shaw

○ ○ ○ ○ ○

The real questions are the ones that obtrude upon your consciousness whether you like it or not, the ones that make your mind start vibrating like a jackhammer, the ones that you "come to terms with" only to discover that they are still there. The real questions refuse to be placated. They barge into your life at the times when it seems most important for them to stay away. They are the questions asked most frequently and answered most inadequately, the ones that reveal their true natures slowly, reluctantly, most often against your will.

—Ingrid Bengis

Do you "research" it? The heart cools off at the word.

—Howard Nemerov

Now those guys can sit naked in the snow at 18,000 feet, and they have such powers of men-

tal discipline that if they put their mind to it, hell, they can generate enough heat to melt snow for twenty feet around. Now you put that Tibetan priest on the mound, naked or not, with a baseball in his palm, and he'll take that power of concentration and make the ball disappear and then materialize down the line in the catcher's mitt. *There's* my idea of a relief pitcher.

—Bill Lee

The reason we like precious jewels so much is they remind us of planes of consciousness we've lived on where those are the pebbles.

—Aldous Huxley

I'd call it love if love
didn't take so many years
But lust too is a jewel. . . .

—Adrienne Rich

It is eternity now. I am in the midst of it. It is about me in the sunshine.

—Richard Jefferies

Fortunate are the nations that can build wooden houses. Because wood breathes, transforms, deteriorates, like us. It is also important to have flowers and plants where we live, because they breathe, too. Contemplating a flower for three seconds can be a captivating solitary journey back to original geometry, which is always revitalizing.

—Henry Skolimowski

One night when my two-and-a-half-year-old granddaughter was staying with me . . . we were at home taking a bubble bath together and singing, "Here we are taking a bubble bath, a bubble bath," etc. All of a sudden, no one was singing and I experienced both of us looking deeply into each other's eyes and there was no sound at all. It lasted but a few moments and I felt shivers up my spine. That was intimacy.

—Lynn Moore
Pilgrimage magazine

I always saw better when my eyes were closed.

—Tom Waits

I remember a small sharp disappointment on the death of a pet rabbit. It developed a growth in the jaw and was sent to the vet to be killed. This was explained to me and I was reconciled to its loss. But the vet on his own initiative decided to operate. He sent the animal back a week later, pronouncing it cured. I greeted it ecstatically and it died that night.

—Evelyn Waugh
A Little Learning

. . . Between grief and nothing I will take grief.

—William Faulkner
The Wild Palms

Windows listen for announcements of broken glass.

—Source unknown
Quoted in Richard Kehl's
Silver Departures

A boy named Eddie Shell came one afternoon to play with Frank and me, and at the hour for going home did not know how to do so. This is a malady that afflicts all children, but my mother was not sure how she should handle it in Eddie's case. She consulted us secretly as to whether he should be asked to stay for supper; we thought not, so she hinted to him that his mother might be expecting him. He was so slow in acting upon the hint that we were all in despair and began to feel guilty because we had not pressed him to stay. What I remember now is Eddie standing at last on the other side of the screen door and trying to say goodbye as if he meant it. My mother said warmly, "Well, Eddie, come and see us again." Whereupon he opened the door and walked in.

—Mark Van Doren
The Autobiography Of Mark Van Doren

○ ○ ○ ○ ○

Worshipping the teapot instead of drinking the tea.

—Wei Wu Wei

When we think we're separate, we lose power. Whenever I say "my," I have lost my power. Power is not *my* power; it is not enlarging oneself as a separate individual. It is only gainable as part of a larger whole. Then you communicate with the rest of yourself—which may be a tree. You, reciprocally, are moved by the universe. Whenever you shut down connectedness, you get depressed. Psychic awareness breaks in as a gift. It's fearful to know we're connected to everything in the universe, because then we're responsible.

—Glenda Taylor
We Are The Web

We milk the cow of the world, and as we do
We whisper in her ear, "You are not true."
                                    —Richard Wilbur

A cover of darkness, separation, and confusion are necessary prerequisites for the eventual rebirth of a lost and wandering soul.
                                    —Nor Hall
                        The Moon And The Goddess

Lord, hear me out, and hear me out this day:
From me to Thee's a long and terrible way.
                                    —Theodore Roethke

I am simply a human being, more or less.
                                    —Saul Bellow
                                            Herzog

A memory of love disguised as a meadow. . . .
                                    —Vladimir Nabokov

"It came to me . . . that when people fall in love they entrust to each other the idea of themselves."

"Do you mean their own idea of themselves?"

"I mean the essential idea of them that perhaps they don't even know themselves. Each holds out to the other this obscure and unknown thing for the other to perceive and keep safe."
                                    —Russell Hoban
                            The Medusa Frequency

Eternity is not the hereafter. Eternity has nothing to do with time. . . . This is it. If you don't get it here, you won't get it anywhere. The experience of eternity right here and now is the function of life. Heaven is not the place to have the experience; here's the place to have the experience.

                                    —Joseph Campbell

Abel and Cain met after Abel's death. They were walking in the desert when they recognized each other from afar because they were both very tall. The brothers sat on the ground, lit a fire, and began to eat. They kept silence just like somebody tired at the end of the day. In the sky there shone a star that was still nameless. In the light of the flames, Cain saw the scar of the stone on Abel's forehead and, dropping the piece of bread he was about to eat, begged him to forgive his crime. Abel answered: "Was it you who killed me or was it I who killed you? I do not remember anymore. Here we are sitting together again just like before." Cain said, "Now I know that you have indeed forgiven me because forgetting is forgiving. I will also try to forget." Abel spoke slowly, "That is right. As long as there is remorse, there is guilt."
                                    —Jorge Luis Borges

○ ○ ○ ○ ○

The only real progress lies in learning to be wrong all alone.

                                    —Albert Camus

The answer to helplessness is not so very complicated. A man can do something for peace without having to jump into politics. Each man has inside him a basic decency and goodness. If he listens to it and acts on it, he is giving a great deal of what it is the world needs most. It is not complicated but it takes courage. It takes courage for a man to listen to his own goodness and act on it. Do we dare to be ourselves? This is the question that counts.

—Pablo Casals

We must learn to regard people less in the light of what they do or omit to do, and more in the light of what they suffer.

—Dietrich Bonhoeffer

"A pier," Stephen said. "Yes, a disappointed bridge."

—James Joyce

Freedom of will is the ability to do gladly that which I must do.

—Carl Jung

I was right not to be afraid of any thief but myself, who will end by leaving me nothing.

—Katherine Anne Porter

Just when I found out the meaning of life, they changed it.

—George Carlin

To endure oneself may be the hardest task in the universe.

—Frank Herbert
Dune Messiah

Can we rely on it that a "turning around will be accomplished by enough people quickly enough to save the modern world"? This question is often asked, but whatever answer is given to it will mislead. The answer "yes" would lead to

complacency; the answer "no" to despair. It is desirable to leave these perplexities behind us and get down to work.

—E.F. Schumacher
A Guide For The Perplexed

"How are you?"

"Perfect, thank you. I'm traveling incognito."

"Oh? As what are you disguised?"

"I am disguised as myself."

"Don't be silly. That's no disguise. That's what you are."

"On the contrary, it must be a very good disguise, for I see it has fooled you completely."

—Nasrudin
Sufi Tales

Instead of hating the people you think are warmakers, hate the appetites and the disorder in your own soul, which are the causes of war.

—Thomas Merton

It is no use walking anywhere to preach unless our walking is our preaching.

—St. Francis of Assisi

Once his brother asked Ryokan to visit his house and speak to his delinquent son. Ryokan came but did not say a word of admonition to the boy. He stayed overnight and prepared to leave the next morning. As the wayward nephew was lacing up Ryokan's sandals, he felt a drop of warm water. Glancing up, he saw

Ryokan looking down at him, his eyes full of tears. Ryokan then returned home, and the nephew changed for the better.

—John Stevens
One Rose, One Bowl

○ ○ ○ ○ ○

There's nothing wrong with the world. What's wrong is our way of looking at it.

—Henry Miller
Big Sur, And The Oranges Of Hieronymus Bosch

. . . That's the main business of the poem!—to see if you can't make up a language that sets all your selves talking at once—all of them being fair to each other.

—Richard Wilbur

Good lovers have known for centuries that the hand is probably the primary sex organ.

—Eleanor Hamilton

To fall in love is to create a religion that has a fallible God.

—Jorge Luis Borges

The bed must always be a beautiful place, not only because you make love there but because you dream there as well.

—Anaïs Nin

Actually, however, there is no cause to recoil from the "historian" tag. Hardly a pure science, history is closer to animal husbandry than it is to mathematics in that it involves selective breeding. The principle difference between the husbandryman and the historian is that the former breeds sheep or cows or such and the latter breeds (assumed) facts. The husbandryman uses his skills to enrich the future, the historian uses his to enrich the past. Both are usually up to their ankles in bullshit.

—Tom Robbins
Another Roadside Attraction

Your friends will know you better in the first minute you meet than your acquaintances will know you in a thousand years.

—Richard Bach
Illusions

There are many objects of desire, and therefore many desires. Some are born with us, hunger, yearning, and pride of place, and some are of the foolishness of the world, such as the desire to eat off silver plates. Desire is a wild horse to be tamed. Virtue is habit long continued. The taming of desire is like the training of the athlete. Discipline is not the restraint but the use of energy. . . . When I forbid myself what I may have, no man is going to tempt me with what is truly forbidden.

—Guy Davenport

It is like coming across a light in thick darkness; it is like receiving treasure in poverty. The four elements and the five aggregates are no more felt as burdens; so light, so easy, so free are you. Your very existence has been delivered from all limitations; you have become open, light, and transparent.

—Yuan-Wu

There are no true beginnings but in pain. When you understand that and can withstand pain, then you're almost ready to start.

—Leslie Woolf Hedley

If you don't chew your food, who will?

—Sign on the wall
Royal American Restaurant, Oakland, California

Why does man kill? He kills for food. And not only for food. Frequently, there must be a beverage.

—Woody Allen

O O O O O

Transcendence or detachment, leaving the body, pure love, lack of jealousy—that's the vision we are given in our culture, generally, when we think of the highest thing. . . . Another way to look at it is that the aim of the person is not to be detached, but to be more attached—to be attached to working; to be attached to making chairs or something that helps everyone; to be attached to beauty; to be attached to music.

—Robert Bly

It's linkage I'm talking about,
       and harmonies and structures
And all the various things that lock
       our wrists to the past.

—Charles Wright

In the people's eyes, in the swing, tramp, and trudge; in the bellow and uproar; the carriages, motor cars, omnibuses, vans, sandwich men shuffling and swinging; brass bands; barrel organs; in the triumph and the jingle and the strange high singing of some airplane overhead was what she loved; life; London, this moment in June.

—Virginia Woolf
Mrs. Dalloway

I only talk about writing in the most mechanical fashion: good habits, bad habits, how to know when you're working right, how to know when you're working wrong. I almost never like to think about the aim. I assume the aim just comes out of the deepest part of your consciousness, if you're serious about the job. There are purposes you can state, but it could be misleading to talk about them, because there are other deeper purposes that you can't state.

—Norman Mailer

The life of simplicity is simple, but it opens to us a book in which we never get beyond the first syllable.

—Dag Hammarskjöld

For us, there is only the trying. The rest is not our business.

—T.S. Eliot
"East Coker"

The community stagnates without the impulse of the individual. The impulse dies away without the sympathy of the community.

—William James

That was the first time it occurred to me that all my life I had feared imprisonment, the nun's cell, the hospital bed, the places where one faced the self without distraction, without the crutches of other people.

—Edna O'Brien
The Love Object

Take away love and our earth is a tomb.

—Robert Browning

Nobody expects a man and a woman to reach the same corner at the same time.

—Marta Lynch
Latin Lover

Despite the light's unusual manifestation, however, not one person has expressed any doubt whatsoever that it was a being, a being of light. Not only that, it is a personal being. It has a very definite personality. The love and warmth which emanate from this being to the dying person are utterly beyond words, and he feels completely surrounded by it and taken up in it, completely at ease and accepted in the presence of this being.

—Raymond A. Moody, Jr.
Life After Life

Just know your lines and don't bump into the furniture.

—Spencer Tracy

○ ○ ○ ○ ○

When shall we open our minds to the conviction that the ultimate reality of the world is neither matter nor spirit, is no definite thing, but a perspective? God is perspective and hierarchy; Satan's sin was an error of perspective. Now, a perspective is perfected by the multiplication of its viewpoints and the precision with which we react to each one of its planes. The intuition of higher values fertilizes our contact with the lesser ones, and love for what is near and small makes the sublime real and effective within our hearts.

—José Ortega y Gasset

For death remembered should be like a mirror
Who tells us life's but breath, to trust it error.

—William Shakespeare

Seeing death as the end of life is like seeing the horizon as the end of the ocean.

—David Searls

To know how little one knows is to have genuine knowledge.

Not to know how little one knows is to be deluded.

Only he who knows when he is deluded can free himself from such delusion. The intelligent man is not deluded, because he knows and accepts his ignorance as ignorance, and thereby has genuine knowledge.

—Lao-tzu

Ignorance has no beginning, but it has an end. There is a beginning but no end to knowledge.

—B.K.S. Iyengar
Light On Yoga

Life leads the thoughtful man on a path of many
    windings.
Now the course is checked, now it runs straight
    again.
Here winged thoughts may pour freely forth in
    words,
There the heavy burden of knowledge must be
    shut away in silence.
But when two people are at one in their inmost
    hearts,
They shatter even the strength of iron or of
    bronze.
And when two people understand each other in
    their inmost hearts,
Their words are sweet and strong, like the fra-
    grance of orchids.

—Confucius

It is a good thing, it is even salutary, for a child to have periods of boredom, for him to learn to know the dialectics of exaggerated play and causeless, pure boredom.

—Gaston Bachelard

Work is love made visible. And if you cannot work with love but only with distaste, it is better that you should leave your work and sit at the gate of the temple and take alms of those who work with joy. For if you bake bread with indifference, you bake a bitter bread that feeds but half man's hunger.

—Kahlil Gibran
The Prophet

I died from minerality and became vegetable;
And from vegetativeness I died and became
    animal.
I died from animality and became man.
Then why fear disappearance through death?
Next time I shall die
Bringing forth wings and feathers like angels;
After that, soaring higher than angels—
What you cannot imagine,
I shall be that.

—Jelaluddin Rumi

○ ○ ○ ○ ○

What friends really mean to each other can be demonstrated better by the exchange of a magic ring or a horn than by psychology.

—Hugo von Hofmannsthal

Our lives are also fed by kind words and gracious behavior. We are nourished by expressions like "excuse me," and other such simple courtesies. Our spirits are also richly fed on compliments and praise, nourished by consideration as well as whole wheat bread. Rudeness, the absence of the sacrament of consideration, is but another mark that our time-is-money society is lacking in spirituality, if not also in its enjoyment of life.

—Ed Hays

Friendships begun in this world will be taken up again, never to be broken off.

—St. Francis de Sales

We begin life with the world presenting itself to us as it is. Someone—our parents, teachers, analysts—hypnotizes us to "see" the world and construe it in the "right" way. These others label the world, attach names and give voices to the beings and events in it, so that thereafter, we cannot read the world in any other language or hear it saying other things to us. The task is to break the hypnotic spell, so that we become undeaf, unblind, and multilingual, thereby letting the world speak to us in new voices and write all its possible meaning in the new book of our existence. Be careful in your choice of hypnotists.

—Sidney Jourard

There is nothing wrong with you.
Anyone who says something
is wrong   is wrong.

—Renais Jeanne Hill

And if you can be compassionate and not revolted by anything you see so you can give people just, exact, unemotional information on the nature of their subconscious, you can help them become more sane.

—Stephen Gaskin

Love has no claims. Love has no expectations. Most of us were raised to become prostitutes. We have the illusion that with good behavior, good grades, lots of awards, pretty clothes, nice smiles, we can buy love. How many ifs were you raised with? I love you if you make it through high school. I love you if you bring good grades home. Boy, would I love you if I could say my son is a doctor. You become a doctor or a lawyer, or whatever your parents never were able to become, with the illusion that they will love you more. Love can never be bought. There are people who spend their lives prostituting themselves, pleasing other people in the hope of getting love. They will shop the rest of their lives for it and they will never find it.

—Elisabeth Kübler-Ross

It came to me that reform should begin at home, and since that day I have not had time to remake the world.

—Will Durant

I believe that the first test of a truly great man is his humility. I do not mean by humility, doubt of his own powers. But really great men have a curious feeling that the greatness is not in them, but through them. And they see something divine in every other man.

—John Ruskin

I destroy my enemy by making him my friend.

—Abraham Lincoln

No one has ever loved anyone the way everyone wants to be loved.

—Mignon McLaughlin

O O O O O

. . . (Gertrude Stein) died firmly in character, having delivered from her hospital bed the last specimen and one of the most searching and comical specimens of Steinese. "What is the answer?" she inquired, and getting no answer, said laughing, "In that case, what is the question?"

—F.W. Dupee
Selected Writings Of Gertrude Stein

We do not walk on our legs, but on our Will.

—Sufi proverb

The most perplexing form of evil, and especially so for all idealists, is that kind of evil which comes out of our efforts to do good. Perhaps when we try to do good without love, we create evil.

—William Irwin Thompson

Everyone takes the limits of his own vision for the limits of the world.

—Arthur Schopenhauer

I . . . doubt that film can ever argue effectively against its own material: that a genuine anti-war film, say, can be made on the basis of even the ugliest battle scenes. . . . No matter what film-makers intend, film always argues yes. People have been modeling their lives after films for years, but the medium is somehow unsuited to moral lessons, cautionary tales, or polemics of any kind. If you want to make a pacifist film, you must make an exemplary film about peaceful men.

—Renata Adler
A Year In The Dark

A prophecy that comes true, especially a negative prophecy, is a prophecy that has failed. One doesn't prophesy for the purpose of being accurate. A prophecy is an attempt to warn or to prepare people to make a change, and if they make that change, then what they're preparing for just may not occur.

—Paul Solomon

The epitome of the human realm is to be stuck in a huge traffic jam of discursive thought.

—Chögyam Trungpa
The Myth Of Freedom

The intelligent man who is proud of his intelligence is like the condemned man who is proud of his large cell.

—Simone Weil

The man in whom Tao
Acts without impediment
Does not bother with his own interests
And does not despise
Others who do.
He does not struggle to make money
And does not make a virtue of poverty.
He goes his way
Without relying on others
And does not pride himself
On walking alone.
While he does not follow the crowd
He won't complain of those who do.
Rank and reward
Make no appeal to him;
Disgrace and shame
Do not deter him.
He is not always looking
For right and wrong
Always deciding "Yes" or "No."

—Thomas Merton
The Way Of Chuang Tzu

What am I doing at a level of consciousness where this is real?

—Thaddeus Golas
The Lazy Man's Guide To Enlightenment

○ ○ ○ ○ ○

My own habitual feeling is that the world is so extremely odd, and everything in it so surprising. Why *should* there be green grass and liquid water, and *why* have I got hands and feet?

—Don John Chapman

Since everything is but an apparition, perfect in being what it is, having nothing to do with good or bad, acceptance or rejection, one may well burst out in laughter.

—Longchenpa

To describe happiness is to diminish it.

—Henri Stendhal

In later life, as in earlier, only a few persons influence the formation of our character; the multitude pass us by like a distant army. One friend, one teacher, one beloved, one club, one dining table, one work table are the means by which his nation and the spirit of his nation affect the individual.

—Jean Paul Richter

How people keep correcting us when we are young! There's always some bad habit or other they tell us we ought to get over. Yet most bad habits are tools to get us through life.

—Johann Wolfgang von Goethe

The *shlemiel* lands on his back and bruises his nose.

—Yiddish proverb

The trouble about arguments is, they ain't nothing but theories, after all, and theories don't prove nothing, they only give you a place to rest on a spell when you are tuckered out butting around and around trying to find out something there ain't no way *to* find out.

—Mark Twain

What had happened? Nothing particularly original. We had a fight, our first, nothing more or less annihilating than that. What had overcharged the rhetoric and ignited the resentment was of course her role of mother's daughter rubbing against mine of father's son—our first fight hadn't even been ours. But then the battle initially rocking most marriages is usually just that—fought by surrogates for real antagonists whose conflict is never rooted in the here and now but sometimes originates so far back that all that remains of the grandparents' values are the newlyweds' ugly words. Virginal they may wish to be, but the worm in the dream is always the past, that impediment to all renewal.

—Philip Roth
The Counterlife

We are the echo of the future.

—W.S. Merwin

The great mistake of the Marxists and of the whole of the nineteenth century was to think that by walking straight on, one mounted upward into the air.

—Simone Weil

SUNBEAMS

Truth is beautiful, without doubt; and so are lies.

—Ralph Waldo Emerson

The things of mine that are utterly lost are the ones that, when I lost them, were not found by someone else.

—Antonio Porchia

Sit, walk, or run, but don't wobble.

—Zen proverb

There is no skeptic who does not feel that men have doubted before, but no man who is in love thinks that anyone has been in love before.

—G.K. Chesterton

Love had brought her here, to lie beside this young man; love was the key to every good; love lay like a mirage through the golden gates of sex.

—Doris Lessing
A Proper Marriage

○ ○ ○ ○ ○

One does not become enlightened by imagining figures of light, but by making the darkness conscious.

—Carl Jung

All you hear from guys is desire, desire, desire, knocking its way out of the breast, and fear, striking and striking. Enough already! Time for a word of truth. Time for something notable to be heard. Otherwise, accelerating like a stone,

you fall from life to death. Exactly like a stone, straight into deafness, and till the last repeating *I want I want I want*, then striking the earth and entering it forever!

—Saul Bellow
Henderson The Rain King

The great function of poetry is to give back to us the situations of our dreams.

—Gaston Bachelard

"The question is," said Alice, "whether you *can* make words mean so many different things."

"The question is," said Humpty Dumpty, "which is to be master—that's all."

—Lewis Carroll
Through The Looking Glass

Marriage is not a matter of creating a quick community of spirit by tearing down and destroying all boundaries, but rather a good marriage is that in which each appoints the other guardian of his solitude. . . . Once the realization is accepted that even between the closest human beings infinite distances continue to exist, a wonderful living side by side can grow up, if they succeed in loving the distance between them no less than one another.

—Rainer Maria Rilke

What is more beautiful than a road? It is the symbol and the image of an active, varied life.

—George Sand

Monetary donations to a spiritual cause, contributions of physical labor, involvement with a particular guru, none of these necessarily

123

mean that we have actually committed ourselves to openness. More likely these kinds of commitments are simply ways of proving that we have joined the side of "right."

—Chögyam Trungpa

Silence makes me nervous 'cause he doesn't come or go. He just hangs around with his hands in his pockets.

—J.R. Slaughter

○ ○ ○ ○ ○

Trouble is a part of your life, and if you don't share it, you don't give the person who loves you enough chance to love you enough.

—Dinah Shore

Even the promiscuous feel pain.

—Warren Beatty

Success can make you go one of two ways—it can make you a prima donna, or it can smooth the edges, take away the insecurities, let the nice things come out.

—Barbara Walters

I decided to start anew—to strip away what I had been taught, to accept as true my own thinking. This was one of the best times of my life. There was no one around to look at what I was doing, no one interested, no one to say anything about it one way or another. I was alone and singularly free, working into my own, unknown—no one to satisfy but myself. I began with charcoal and paper and decided not to use any color until it was impossible to do what I wanted to do in black and white. I believe it was June before I needed blue.

—Georgia O'Keefe

Some things you must always be unable to bear. Some things you must never stop refusing to bear. Injustice and outrage and dishonor and shame. No matter how young you are or how old you have got. Not for kudos and not for cash. Your picture in the paper nor money in the bank, neither. Just refuse to bear them.

—William Faulkner

Part of me is still waiting to grow up, to be an adult, and the other part knows there is no such thing.

—Richard Dreyfuss

Sometimes, Lord, one is tempted to say that if you wanted us to behave like the lilies of the field you might have given us an organization more like theirs. But that, I suppose, is just your grand experiment. Or no; not an experiment, for you have no need to find things out. Rather your grand enterprise. To make an organism which is also a spirit; to make that terrible oxymoron, a "spiritual animal." To take a poor primate, a beast with nerve endings all over it, a creature with a stomach that wants to be filled, a breeding animal that wants its mate, and say, "Now get on with it. Become a god."

—C.S. Lewis
A Grief Observed

It's a risky thing to pray and the danger is that our very prayers get between God and us. The great thing in prayer is not to pray, but to go directly to God. . . . The fact is, however, that if you descend into the depths of your own spirit . . . and arrive somewhere near the center of what you are, you are confronted with the inescapable truth that, at the very root of your existence, you are in constant and immediate contact with the infinite power of God.

—Thomas Merton

Life shrinks or expands according to one's courage.

—Anaïs Nin

It is one of the most beautiful compensations of this life that no man can sincerely try to help another without helping himself.

—Ralph Waldo Emerson

To the blind pen the hand that writes is unreal, its writing unmeaning.

—Rabindranath Tagore

One windy day two monks were arguing about a flapping banner. The first said, "I say the banner is moving, not the wind." The second said, "I say the wind is moving, not the banner." A third monk passed by and said, "The wind is not moving. The banner is not moving. Your minds are moving."

—Zen parable

All who seek the roots of life dig in solitude for them.

—C.H.A. Bjerregaard

○ ○ ○ ○ ○

That is what learning is. You suddenly understand something you've understood all your life, but in a new way. There's a pressure on us all the time to go on to something that seems new because there are new words attached to it. But I want to take words as ordinary as bread. Or life. Or death. Cliches. I want to have my nose rubbed in cliches.

—Doris Lessing
The Four-Gated City

I leave this world without a regret.

—Henry David Thoreau
last words

Turn up the lights. I don't want to go home in the dark.

—O. Henry
last words

It requires moral courage to grieve; it requires religious courage to rejoice.

—Sören Kierkegaard

Let us face a pluralistic world in which there are no universal churches, no single remedy for all diseases, no one way to teach or write or sing, no magic diet, no world poets, and no chosen races, but only the wretched and wonderfully diversified human race.

—Jacques Barzun

Every individual is representative of the whole . . . and should be intimately understood, and this would give a far greater understanding of mass movements and sociology.

—Anaïs Nin

But as she has grown, her smile has widened with a touch of fear and her glance has taken on depth. Now she is aware of some of the losses you incur by being here—the extraordinary rent you have to pay as long as you stay.

—Annie Dillard

Lonely people talking to each other can make each other lonelier.

—Lillian Hellman
The Autumn Garden

Between no place of mine and no place of yours, you'd have thought I'd know the way by now.

—W.S. Merwin

I never dreamed of being Shakespeare or Goethe, and I never expected to hold the great mirror of truth up before the world; I dreamed only of being a little pocket mirror, the sort that a woman can carry in her purse; one that reflects small blemishes, and some great beauties, when held close enough to the heart.

—Peter Altenberg

Mirror makers know the secret
—one does not make a mirror
to resemble a person.
One brings a person to the mirror.

—Jack Spicer

Then there is the matter of my mother's abandonment of me. Again, this is the common experience. They walk ahead of us, and walk too fast, and forget us, they are so lost in thoughts of their own, and soon or late they disappear. The only mystery is that we expect it to be otherwise.

—Marilynne Robinson

I stand on the terrible threshold, and I see
The end and the beginning in each other's
     arms.

—Stanley Kunitz
"Open The Gates"

If God lived on earth, people would break his windows.

—Yiddish proverb

Have you seen a room from which faith has gone, like a marriage from which love has gone? And patience, patience everywhere like a fog.

—Graham Greene

And all the time it's your own story, even when you think—"It's all just made up, a trick. What is the author trying to do?" Reader, we are in such a story: all of this is trying to arrange a kind of prayer for you. Pray for me.

—William Stafford

○ ○ ○ ○ ○

Kindness is more important than wisdom, and the recognition of this is the beginning of wisdom.
— Theodore Isaac Rubin

How hard it is to escape from places! However carefully one goes, they hold you—you leave little bits of yourself fluttering on the fences, little rags and shreds of your very life.
— Katherine Mansfield

There is no stopping place in this life—nor is there ever one for any man, no matter how far along his way he's gone.
— Meister Eckhart

God is always opening his hand.
— Spanish proverb

God is more glorified by a man who uses the good things of this life in simplicity and with gratitude than by the nervous asceticism of someone who is agitated about every detail of his self-denial. . . . His [the latter's] struggle for perfection becomes a kind of battle of wits with the Creator who made all things good.
— Thomas Merton

Why do you assume that an existence that does not succeed in taking root or bearing fruit in the form of a tangible work is less valuable than another? Why might not the world, which has need for stable families and settled people, need also these mobiles and wandering creatures whose action takes the form of series of seem- ingly unrelated trials or tests cutting across all kinds of areas? . . . We must, to a certain extent, look for a stable port, but if Life keeps tearing us away, not letting us settle anywhere, this in itself may be a call and a benediction.
— Pierre Teilhard de Chardin

Love from one being to another can only be that two solitudes come nearer, recognize and protect and comfort each other.
— Han Suyin

What a lovely surprise to finally discover how unlonely being alone can be.
— Ellen Burstyn

You must do the thing you think you cannot do.
— Eleanor Roosevelt

And then, not expecting it, you become middle-aged and anonymous. No one notices you. You achieve a wonderful freedom. It is a positive thing. You can move about, unnoticed and invisible.
— Doris Lessing

All the powers work so that you should come to a bad ending, but our soul works for the opposite—that the ending should be good. Actually, the ending is always good.
— Isaac Bashevis Singer

○ ○ ○ ○ ○

The best form is to worship God in every form.
— Neem Karoli Baba

Don't think twice, it's all right.

—Bob Dylan

I came from brilliancy
and return to
brilliancy.
What is this?

—Zen poem

After the rain, good weather.

In the wink of an eye, the universe throws off
its muddy clothes.

—Ho Chi Minh

There is in all things an inexhaustible sweetness
and purity, a silence that is a fountain of action
and joy. It rises up in wordless gentleness and
flows out to me from unseen roots of all created
being.

—Thomas Merton

Without trust, words become the hollow sound
of a wooden gong. With trust, words become
life itself.

—John Harold

Siddhartha listened. He was now listening
intently, completely absorbed, quite empty, taking in everything. . . . He could no longer distinguish the different voices—the merry voice
from the weeping voice, the childish voice from
the manly voice. They all belonged to each
other. . . . They were all interwoven and inter-
locked, entwined in a thousand ways. And all
the voices, all the goals, all the yearnings, all
the sorrows, all the pleasures, all the good and
evil, all of them together was the world. All of
them together was the stream of events, the
music of life . . . when he did not listen to the
sorrow or laughter, when he did not bind his
soul to any one particular voice and absorb it
in his Self, but heard them all, the whole, the
unity, then the great song of a thousand voices
consisted of one word: Om—perfection.

—Hermann Hesse
Siddhartha

I want a dime, if you can spare a dime. I'll go
along my way peacefully—if you can't I'll go
along my way peacefully—ya can't win—ya
can't lose—and between here and Bismark,
Idaho I got nothin' but lost and lost and lost
everything I had.

—Jack Kerouac
Railroad Earth

The trouble with superheroes is what to do
between phone booths.

—Ken Kesey

When your mind becomes demanding, when
you long for something, you will end up violat-
ing your own precepts: not to tell lies, not to
steal, not to kill, not to be immoral, and so
forth. If you keep your original mind, the precepts will keep themselves.

—Suzuki Roshi
Zen Mind, Beginner's Mind

Your end, which is endless, is as a snowflake
dissolving in the pure air.

—Buddhist saying

Keep on sowing your seed, for you never know
which will grow—perhaps it all will.

—*Ecclesiastes* 11:6

Vision brings a new appreciation of what there is. It makes a person see things differently, rather than see different things. After all nobody can ever escape Being, least of all his own being. It is the vision that gives meaning to our experiences and our actions by making us face the problem, and therefore also vision alone gives man a sense of direction and enables him to sketch a map which will guide him in his task of finding himself rather than running away from himself.

—Herbert Guenther

The way is not in the sky. The way is in the heart.

—*Dhammapada*

Our life is an apprenticeship to the truth that around every circle another can be drawn; that there is no end in nature, but every end is a beginning, and under every deep a lower deep opens.

—Ralph Waldo Emerson

Make a bigger space in the universe for your head to live in and it will grow to fill the space.

—David Crosby

A man needs a little madness or else he never dares to cut the rope and be free.

—Nikos Kazantzakis
Zorba The Greek

Friend . . . GOOD.

—Frankenstein monster
James Whale's *The Bride Of Frankenstein*

○ ○ ○ ○ ○

The strength, vitality, and effectiveness of thought is seldom considered. Thought, you may say, will not stop a war—yet what do you think *started* such a war? Throughout history the downtrodden have often risen into power, using force, rebelling against their oppressors; and yet, learning little from that experience, they turn and become the *new* elite, the *new* power-holders. Their physical conditions may be completely changed. Now theirs, the offices of government, the wealth. Gone are the conditions that, it would seem, caused the uprising. Yet in retaliation they strike out, forming a new class of downtrodden who must in *their* turn rise and retaliate.

Despite all appearances, conditions of an exterior nature do not cause wars, or poverty, or disease, or any of the unfortunate circumstances apparent in the world. Your beliefs form your reality. Your thoughts generate practical experience. When these change, conditions will change.

—Seth
Jane Roberts' *The Nature Of The Psyche*

Whatever the self describes, describes the self.

—Jacob Boehme

We love when this man Ulysses comes back in disguise for his revenge. But suppose he forgot what he came back for and just sat around day in, day out in the disguise. This happens to many a frail spirit who forgets what the disguises are for, doesn't understand complexity or how to return to simplicity. From telling different things to everyone, he forgets what the case is originally and what he wants himself. How rare is simple thought and pureheartedness! Even a moment of pureheartedness I bow down to, down to the ground.

—Saul Bellow

I try to give to the poor people for love what the rich could get for money. No, I wouldn't touch a leper for a thousand pounds, yet I willingly cure him for the love of God.

—Mother Theresa

Not only should you believe in what you are doing, but you should know what you are doing.

—Mason Williams

The degree of freedom from unwanted thoughts and the degree of concentration on a single thought are the measures to gauge spiritual progress.

—Ramana Maharshi

Centering: that act which precedes all others on the potter's wheel. The bringing of the clay into a spinning, unwobbling pivot, which will then be free to take innumerable shapes as potter and clay press against each other. The firm, tender, sensitive pressure which yields as much as it asserts. It is like a handclasp between two living hands, receiving the greeting at the very moment they give it. It is this speech between the hand and the clay that makes me think of dialogue. And it is a language far more interesting than the spoken vocabulary which tries to describe it, for it is spoken not by the tongue and lips but by the whole body, by the whole person, speaking and listening.

And with listening too, it seems to me, it is not the ear that hears, it is not the physical organ that performs that act of inner receptivity. It is the total person who hears. Sometimes the skin seems to be the best listener, as it prickles and thrills, say to a sound or a silence; or the fantasy, the imagination: how it bursts into inner pictures as it listens and then responds by pressing its language, its forms, into the listening clay. To be open to what we hear, to be open in what we say. . . .

—M.C. Richards
Centering

Love that ends is the shadow of love; true love is without beginning or end.

—Hazrat Inayat Khan

The Kingdom of Heaven is within you. . . . Seek ye first the Kingdom of Heaven and all things will be added unto you.

—Jesus

Miracles occur naturally as expressions of love. The real miracle is the love that inspires them. In this sense everything that comes from love is a miracle.

—*A Course In Miracles*

○ ○ ○ ○ ○

You have everything in you that Buddha has, that Christ has. You've got it all. But only when you start to acknowledge it is it going to get interesting. Your problem is you're afraid to acknowledge your own beauty. You're too busy holding on to your own unworthiness. You'd rather be a schnook sitting before some great man. That fits in more with who you think you are. Well, enough already. I sit before you and I look and I see your beauty, even if you don't.

—Ram Dass
Grist For The Mill

. . . As long as Christ knew I wasn't a sissy, I had nothing to fear.

—Tiny Tim

A drunken man who falls out of a cart, though he may suffer, does not die. His bones are the same as other people's; but he meets his accident in a different way. His spirit is in a condition of security. He is not conscious of riding in the cart; neither is he conscious of falling out of it. Ideas of life, death, fear and the like cannot penetrate his breast; and so he does not suffer from contact with objective existence. If such security is to be got from wine, how much more is it to be got from God?

—Chuang Tzu

The seed of God is in us. Given an intelligent and hard-working farmer, it will thrive and grow up to God, whose seed it is; and accordingly its fruits will be God-nature. Pear seeds grow into pear trees, nut seeds into nut trees, and God seed into God.

—Meister Eckhart

It is within my power either to serve God, or not to serve Him. Serving Him I add to my own good and the good of the whole world. Not serving Him, I forfeit my own good and deprive the world of that good, which was in my power to create.

—Leo Tolstoy

Stained glass, engraved glass, frosted glass; give me plain glass.

—John Fowles

You do not need to leave your room. . . . Remain sitting at your table and listen. Do not even listen, simply wait. Do not even wait, be quite still and solitary. The world will freely offer itself to you to be unmasked. It has no choice. It will roll in ecstasy at your feet.

—Franz Kafka

Prayer and love are learned in the hour
when prayer becomes impossible
and your heart has turned to stone.

—Thomas Merton

Don't goof off.

—Suzuki Roshi

To feel life is meaningless unless "I" can be permanent is like having desperately fallen in love with an inch.

—Alan Watts

Love is all fire; and so heaven and hell are the same place.

—Norman O. Brown

○ ○ ○ ○ ○

The soul of every man does possess the power of learning the truth, and the organ to see it with. . . . Just as one might have to turn the whole body round in order that the eye should see the light instead of the darkness, so the entire soul must be turned away from this changing world until its eye can bear to contemplate reality.

—Plato

In a certain sense, every single human soul has more meaning and value than the whole of history.

—Nicholas Berdyaev

Contradiction is the criterion of reality.

—Simone Weil

Fear nothing, for every renewed effort raises all former failures into lessons, all sins into experiences.

—Katherine Tingley

There are no mistakes and it's never boring on the edge of the imagination, which is only pure spirit out having a bit of fun.

—Hugh Romney
aka Wavy Gravy

Salvation is seeing that the universe is good, and becoming a part of that goodness.

—Arthur G. Clutton-Brock

Have courage for the great sorrows of life, and patience for the small ones. And when you have laboriously accomplished your daily task, go to sleep in peace. God is awake.

—Victor Hugo

Whither shall I go from Thy spirit? Or whither shall I flee from Thy presence? If I ascend up into heaven, Thou art there; if I make my bed in hell, behold, Thou art there. If I take the wings of the morning, and dwell in the uttermost parts of the sea: even there shall Thy hand lead me, and Thy right hand shall hold me.

—*Psalms* 139:9

○ ○ ○ ○ ○

The bedroom is one of the most dangerous places in our society. There are more crimes of violence committed there than on the streets of Los Angeles. It's an area with intense anxiety. When sex comes in the door, love flies out the window. Men are afraid of women and women have good reason to be afraid of men. If I hazarded a guess as to the most endemic, prevalent anxiety among human beings—including fear of death, abandonment, loneliness—nothing is more prevalent than the fear of one another.

—R.D. Laing

So long as we read about revolutions in books, they all look very nice—like those landscapes which, as artistic engravings on white vellum, look so pure and friendly: dung heaps engraved on copper do not smell, and the eye can easily wade through an engraved morass.

—Heinrich Heine

We can all remember the catastrophic disappointments we had as children. Looking back, they appear to be trifles, but in childhood—in that moment—it was an agony of suffering. This is because a child is whole, and whole in its reactions; therefore, even if only a toy is taken away from him, it is as though the world were going down. . . . The child within one is the genuine part, and the genuine part within one is that which suffers, that which cannot take reality, or which still reacts in the grown-up person like a child, saying, "I want it all, and if I don't get it, then it is the end of the world. Everything is lost." That is what the genuine kernel of the person remains like and that is the source of suffering. Many grown-ups split off this part and thereby miss individuation, for only if one accepts it and the suffering it imposes on one, can the process of individuation go on.

—Marie-Louise von Franz
Puer Aeternus

We have given the distances birthdays.
—Robert Dana

It is not doing the thing we like to do, but liking the thing we have to do that makes life blessed.
—Johann Wolfgang von Goethe

To those of us who study history not merely as a reminder of man's follies and crimes, but also as an encouraging remembrance of generative souls, the past ceases to be a depressing chamber of horrors; it becomes a celestial city, a spacious country of the mind, wherein a thousand saints, statesmen, inventors, scientists, poets, artists, musicians, lovers, and philosophers still live and speak, teach and carve and sing.
—Will Durant

This path is difficult because it has not been carved; and it has not been carved because I have not lived before.

—Sally Palain

The kind of work we do does not make us holy but we may make it holy. However "sacred" a calling may be, as it is a calling, it has no power to sanctify; but rather as we are and have the divine being within, we bless each task we do, be it eating, or sleeping, or watching, or any other. Whatever they do, who have not much of God's nature, they work in vain.
—Meister Eckhart

A musician must make music, an artist must paint, a poet must write, if he is to be ultimately at peace with himself. What a man can be, he must be.
—Abraham Maslow

Oh lonesome's a bad place
to get crowded into.
—Kenneth Patchen

○ ○ ○ ○ ○

The heart that breaks open can contain the whole universe.
—Joanna Rogers Macy

I saw sorrow turning into clarity.
—Yoko Ono

This is how he went on. And that is how most of us go on, unless we get lucky or rich, unless we take sick and die. We do our work and sometimes it goes well and sometimes it doesn't. And when it doesn't we feel low. We pause for a moment, say a prayer in church, drink a beer under pecans in the backyard, go to a psychiatrist, or smoke some grass if we are young. The granite mass of time cracks and we feel wonder at the world. We go on.

—Chuck Taylor
Always Clear And Simple

There is something in the pang of change,
More than the heart can bear,
Unhappiness remembering happiness.

—Euripides

Every human being is treacherous to every other human being because he has to be true to his own soul.

—D.H. Lawrence

She was weeping over the end of a cycle. How one must be thrust out of a finished cycle in life and that leap the most difficult to make, to part with one's faith, one's love, when one would prefer to renew the faith and recreate the passion. The struggle to emerge out of the past, clean of memories; the inadequacy of our hearts to cut life into separate and final portions; the pain of this constant ambivalence and interrelation of emotions; the hunger for frontiers against which we might lean as upon closed doors before we proceed forward; the struggle against diffusion, new beginnings, against finality in acts without finality or end, in our cursedly repercussive being. . . .

—Anaïs Nin

Hunger is my native place in the land of passions. Hunger for fellowship, hunger for righteousness for a fellowship founded on righteousness, and a righteousness attained in fellowship.

—Dag Hammarskjöld

One must show man not when he's dressed up for Sunday, but in all his phases, his conditions, his base attitudes and spirit—that he goes on, he continues, he has outlived the dinosaur, he has outlived the atom bomb, and I'm convinced in time he can even outlive the wheel.

—William Faulkner

If one can actually revert to the truth, then a great deal of one's suffering can be erased—because a great deal of one's suffering is based on sheer lies.

—R.D. Laing

It is more worthy in the eyes of God . . . if a writer makes three pages sharp and funny about the lives of geese than to make three hundred fat and flabby about God or the American people.

—Garrison Keillor

There is no greater joke than this: that being the Reality ourselves, we seek to gain Reality. We think that there is something binding our Reality and that it must be destroyed before the Reality is gained. It is ridiculous. A day will dawn when you will yourself laugh at your effort. That which is on the day of laughter is also now.

—Ramana Maharshi

○ ○ ○ ○ ○

This "being oneself" is of course impossible. All the talk about it is the expression of collective lostness, confusion, and depression. To say, "I want to be only myself" makes about as much sense as saying, "I want to speak my own language." One has to express himself in the lan-

guage he has grown up with from childhood or has learned since then. One cannot speak his "own" language, and moreover, even if one did, no one else could understand it. Similarly, we cannot find ourselves but only express ourselves through archetypal role enactments, and in this way we may also—perhaps—find ourselves.

—Adolf Guggenbuhl-Craig
Marriage: Dead Or Alive?

The negative has acquired very bad connotations. We say that we should accent the positive; that is a purely male chauvinistic attitude. How would you know you were outstanding unless by contrast there was something instanding? You cannot appreciate the convex without the concave. You cannot appreciate the firm without the yielding.

—Alan Watts
OM: Creative Meditations

When a marriage ends, who is left to understand it?

—Joyce Carol Oates

The man of flesh and blood; the one who is born, suffers and dies—above all, who dies; the man who eats and drinks and plays and sleeps and thinks and wills; the man who is seen and is heard; the brother, the real brother.

—Miguel de Unamuno
The Tragic Sense Of Life

In the dark times
Will there also be singing?
Yes, there will also be singing
About the dark times.

—Bertolt Brecht

I am still of the opinion that only two topics can be of the least interest to a serious and studious mood—sex and the dead.

—William Butler Yeats

Those pleasures so lightly called physical.

—Colette

Artistic growth is, more than it is anything else, a refining of the sense of truthfulness. The stupid believe that to be truthful is easy; only the artist, the great artist, knows how difficult it is.

—Willa Cather

I don't speak with my patients. Only one in a hundred tells the truth. I try to see what I feel when I'm with them, or when I am brought some of their clothing. I have to feel their sickness in my body. This form of healing has nothing to do with books, and can't be learned from another person. It's a matter of feeling, having a fresh mind, knowing how to listen to what no one else listens to.

—Domininga Ñancufil

A broken hand works, but not a broken heart.
—Source unknown

I wish that every human life might be pure transparent freedom.
—Simone de Beauvoir
The Blood Of Others

I travel light; as light,
That is, as a man can travel who will
Still carry his body around because
Of its sentimental value.
—Christopher Fry
The Lady's Not For Burning

Poetry is just the evidence of life. If your life is burning well, poetry is just the ash.
—Leonard Cohen

Good judgement comes from experience. Experience comes from bad judgement.
—Source unknown

O O O O O

Standing on a street corner waiting for no one is Power.
—Gregory Corso
Power

Because all existence is founded upon the ever-present state of union, everything already exists in a state of tranquility. However, this state of tranquility is masked from us by our assumption that there is a separation, that there is a problem.
—Suzuki Roshi

If a pickpocket meets a Holy Man, he will see only his pockets.
—Hari Dass

Row, row, row your boat
Gently down the stream
Merrily, merrily, merrily, merrily
Life is but a dream.
—Traditional

Everyone is in the best seat.
—John Cage

People are never so free with themselves and so recklessly glad as when there is some possibility of commotion or calamity ahead.
—Carson McCullers
The Ballad Of The Sad Cafe

The way to innocence, to the uncreated and to God, leads on, not back, not back to the wolf or to the child, but ever further into sin, ever deeper into human life.
—Hermann Hesse

He who knows nothing loves nothing. He who can do nothing understands nothing. He who understands nothing is worthless. But he who understands also loves, notices, sees. . . . The more knowledge is inherent in a thing, the greater the love. . . . Anyone who imagines that all fruits ripen at the same time as the strawberries knows nothing about grapes.
—Philippus Aureolus Paracelsus

It's a bit hard to bullshit the ocean. It's not listening, you know what I mean.
—David Crosby

When we lay claim to the evil in ourselves, we no longer need fear its occurring outside of our control. For example, a patient comes into therapy complaining that he does not get along well with other people; somehow he always says the wrong thing and hurts their feelings. He is really a nice guy, just has this uncontrollable, neurotic problem. What he does *not* want to know is that his "unconscious hostility" is not his *problem*, it's his *solution*. He is really not a nice guy who wants to be good; he's a bastard who wants to hurt other people while still thinking of himself as a nice guy. If the therapist can guide him into the pit of his own ugly soul, then there may be hope for him. . . . Nothing about ourselves can be changed until it is first accepted.

—Sheldon Kopp
If You Meet The Buddha On the Road, Kill Him

Sometimes a cigar is just a cigar.

—Sigmund Freud

O O O O O

If you are willing to discipline yourself, the physical universe won't need to discipline you.

—Leonard Orr

I have a strong suspicion, but I can't be sure, that much that passes for constant love is a golded-up moment walking in its sleep. Some people know that it is the walk of the dead, but in desperation and desolation, they have staked everything on life after death and the resurrection, so they haunt the graveyard. They build an altar on the tomb and wait there like faithful Mary for the stone to roll away. So the moment has authority over all of their lives. They pray constantly for the miracle of the moment to burst its bond and spread out over time.

—Zora Neale Hurston

A mother is not a person to lean on but a person to make leaning unnecessary.

—Dorothy C. Fisher

And learn power. . . . Be victim to abruptness and seizures, events intercalated, swellings of heart. You'll climb trees. You won't be able to sleep, or need to, for the joy of it. Mornings, when light spreads over the pastures like wings, and fans a secret color into everything, and beats the trees senseless with beauty, so you can't tell whether the beauty is *in* the trees— dazzling in cells like yellow sparks or green flashing water—or *on* them—a transfiguring silver air charged with the wings' invisible motion; mornings you won't be able to walk for the power of it. . . .

—Annie Dillard

Art is the method of levitation, in order to separate one's self from enslavement by the earth.

—Anaïs Nin

Whether or not you can observe a thing depends upon the theory you use. It is the theory which decides what can be observed.

—Albert Einstein

True knowledge is not attained by thinking. It is what you are; it is what you become.

—Sri Aurobindo

In spite of everything I still believe that people are really good at heart.

—Anne Frank

Those that hated goodness are sometimes nearer than those that know nothing at all about it and think they have it already.

—C.S. Lewis

○ ○ ○ ○ ○

Empires rise and fall like the abdomen of God. It's just the universe breathing.

—Scoop Nisker

The good and the wise lead quiet lives.

—Euripides

People have the illusion that all over the world, all the time, all kinds of fantastic things are happening. When in fact, over most of the world, most of the time, nothing is happening.

—David Brinkley

If you help others, you will be helped, perhaps tomorrow, perhaps in one hundred years, but you will be helped. Nature must pay off the debt. . . . It is a mathematical law and all life is mathematics.

—G.I. Gurdjieff

All search for happiness is misery and leads to more misery. The only happiness worth the name is the natural happiness of conscious being.

—Nisargadatta Maharaj

By any precise definition, Washington is a city of advanced depravity. There one meets and dines with the truly great killers of the age, but only the quirkily fastidious are offended, for the killers are urbane and learned gentlemen who discuss their work with wit and charm and know which tool to use on escargots.

—Russell Baker

Some people want to achieve immortality through their work or their descendants. I intend to achieve immortality by not dying.

—Woody Allen

It is but one step from the sublime to the ridiculous.

—Napoleon Bonaparte

Work is life. Not having something to do with one's life, something important or unique to your talents or however you put it, is a bigger killer than cancer.

—Ray Mungo

The deeper the sorrow, the less tongue it has.

—*The Talmud*

When you discover the management, there's nothing to do but go to work for it.

—Hugh Romney

You mustn't force sex to do the work of love or love to do the work of sex.

—Mary McCarthy

Life is what happens to you while you're busy making other plans.

—John Lennon

SUNBEAMS

Turn your face to the sun and the shadows fall behind you.

—Maori proverb

I believe that if you put fine food into a body with a crummy mind, you get a crummy body; but if you put crummy food into a body with expanded awareness, you get a fine body.

—W. Brugh Joy

He was alone in the doorway, digging the street. Bitterness, recriminations, advice, morality, sadness—everything was behind him, and ahead of him was the ragged and ecstatic joy of pure being.

—Jack Kerouac

If the Lord wrote reports like a bureaucrat, Moses would have suffered a terrible hernia lugging those tablets down from the mountain.

—Joel Ponzer

Because demands build up when needs are not admitted, acknowledgement of my needs subjectively, as a factor of my humanity, my dependent creatureliness, will help to prevent these same needs from degenerating into demands for actual fulfillment upon the objective world. Demands ask for fulfillment; needs require only expression.

—James Hillman

○ ○ ○ ○ ○

I would like to see a building—say, the Empire State—I would like to see on one side of it a foot-long strip from top to bottom, with the name of every bricklayer, the name of every electrician, with all the names. So when the guy walked by, he could take his son and say, "See, that's me over there on the forty-fifth floor." Or, "I put the steel beam in." Picasso can point to a painting. I think I've worked harder than Picasso, and what can I point to? A writer can point to a book. Everybody should have something to point to.

Mike Fitzgerald
Interviewed by Studs Terkel

Question: If your house were on fire, which object would you take with you?

Tristan Bernard: The thing nearest the door.

Jean Cocteau: The fire.

—Quoted in *Ballast Quarterly Review*

At around age six, perhaps, I was standing by myself in our front yard waiting for supper, just at that hour in a late summer day when the sun is already below the horizon and the risen full moon in the visible sky stops being chalky and begins to take on light. There comes the moment, and I saw it then, when the moon goes from flat to round. For the first time it met my eyes as a globe. The word "moon" came into my mouth as though fed to me out of a silver spoon. Held in my mouth the moon became a word. It had the roundness of a Concord grape Grandpa took off his vine and gave me to suck out of its skin and swallow whole, in Ohio.

—Eudora Welty
One Writer's Beginnings

139

I remember my grandfather telling me how each of us must live with a full measure of loneliness that is inescapable, and we must not destroy ourselves with our passion to escape this aloneness.

—Jim Harrison
Dalva

This is the true joy of life, the being used up for a purpose recognized by yourself as a mighty one; being a force of nature instead of a feverish, selfish little clod of ailments and grievances, complaining that the world will not devote itself to making you happy. I am of the opinion that my life belongs to the community, and as long as I live, it is my privilege to do for it whatever I can. I want to be thoroughly used up when I die, for the harder I work, the more I live. Life is no "brief candle" to me. It is a sort of splendid torch which I have got hold of for a moment, and I want to make it burn as brightly as possible before handing it on to future generations.

—George Bernard Shaw

My religion is very simple—my religion is kindness.

—Dalai Lama

Fidelity is a matter of perception. . . . Nobody is unfaithful to the sea or to mountains or to death: once recognized, they fill the heart. In love or in terror or in loathing one responds to them with the true self. Fidelity is not an act of the will: the soul is compelled by recognitions. Anyone who loves, anyone who perceives the other person fully, can only be faithful, can never be unfaithful to the sea and the moun-tains and the death in that person, so pitiful and heroic is it to be a human being.

—Russell Hoban
The Medusa Frequency

I'd like to die like this . . .
with the dark fingers of the water
closing and unclosing over these sleepy lights
and a sad bell somewhere murmuring good night.

—Kenneth Patchen
"Crossing On Staten Island Ferry"

Though I have looked everywhere
I can find nothing lowly
in the universe.

—A.R. Ammons
"Still"

Fear tastes like a rusty knife and do not let her into your house. Courage tastes of blood. Stand up straight. Admire the world. Relish the love of a gentle woman. Trust in the Lord.

—John Cheever
The Wapshot Chronicle

All my life I have struggled to make one authen-tic gesture.

—Isadora Duncan

Nobody gets in to see the wizard. Not no way, not no how.

—L. Frank Baum
The Wonderful Wizard Of Oz

○ ○ ○ ○ ○

That so much human struggle seems to take place in sexual terms is somewhat misleading. The ambiguity and uncertainties of fulfilling oneself as a man or as a woman sometimes mask the more profound anguish of simply being human.

—Sheldon Kopp
If You Meet The Buddha On The Road, Kill Him

Looking back, I realize that my loves were, in actuality, obsessions. They caused more pain than pleasure. Sometimes, I can't distinguish between pain and ecstasy.

—Henry Miller

No one is more arrogant toward women, more aggressive or scornful, than the man who is anxious about his virility.

—Simone de Beauvoir
The Second Sex

When a person has been loved early in life, he does not have to try to extract it from sex; sex can be what it is—an intimate relationship between two people who are attracted to each other. Does this mean that sex is something isolated from love? Not necessarily. A well person is not going to run around trying to get everyone in bed. He will want to share his self (and that includes his body) with a person he cares about. But he or she will not preface that relationship with some mystical concept of love. Sex will be a natural outgrowth of a relationship just like anything else. It does not have to be "justified" by love.

—Arthur Janov
The Primal Scream

Never mind. The self is the least of it. Let our scars fall in love.

—Galway Kinnell

We've gone from neurotic sex to reasonably healthy sex and that's really good. And if you're living in the world, sex is a very beautiful part of existence. However, if you in truth want to go to God in this lifetime, then you start to direct your energies toward getting there. The predicament with sexuality is that no matter how nice your intentions are, the act itself is so powerful that it catches you in the gratification that comes from your separateness, which means sensual gratification. And in that sense it's reinforcing your separateness. . . . The game is just to go into the reality where sex is like rubbing sticks together to make a fire. You get to the point where you're already existing in that place where you were having sex to get to.

—Ram Dass
Grist For The Mill

God is voluptuous and delicious.

—Meister Eckhart

Sex is a beast. A large, ugly-beautiful, and potentially very dangerous beast. We defy him at our peril. . . . They say they've observed tiny boy babes, in the womb, with tiny hard-ons. Lust drives us from the start, and will drive us at the end. Little Richard says that it's infectious. And some psychiatric doctors are giving clinics in how to defeat the habit of sex. A habit that can tear up relationships and marriages. I believe!

Here I am saying this, and yet at the very time I am saying this, I am thinking, "When I see a man, a lovely man without clothes—it's like a blow to the gut. It's the same old dumb passion I dealt with thirty years ago." I may get older, but lust never ages. It is the same blow to the belly that it was the first time, a blow so strong and unstoppable that one reels in the wonder of its brute intellect-defeating power.

—Lorenzo W. Milam

We all know that fucking is thus complex and contradictory, that people who can hardly bear each other have sex which is often by mutual consensus sensational, and couples wigged with pot, speed, and the pill fly out on sheer bazazz, "great lovemaking, great!" whereas the nicest love of two fine minds in two fine bodies can come to nothing via fornication—sex is capable of too many a variation, love to some and lust to others! Sex can lead to conception and be as rewarding as cold piss—the world is not filled for nothing with people who have faces like cold piss!—sex can be no more than a transaction for passing mutual use, yet heaven can hit your hip; there is no telling, there is never any telling. . . .

—Norman Mailer
The Prisoner Of Sex

O O O O O

Using another as a means of satisfaction and security is not love. Love is never security; love is a state in which there is no desire to be secure; it is a state of vulnerability.

—J. Krishnamurti

The earth has enough for every man's need, but not for every man's greed.

—Mahatma Gandhi

The most beautiful thing we can experience is the mysterious. It is the source of all true art and science.

—Albert Einstein

If a person works only for himself he can perhaps be a famous scholar, a great wise man, a distinguished poet, but never a complete, genuinely great man. History calls those the greatest . . . who enobled themselves by working for the universal. Experience praises as the most happy the one who made the most people happy.

—Karl Marx

So long as you're struggling, quarreling, there can't be despair. Despair is one of the supreme sins, because a despairing person ceases to struggle. That makes despair the ultimate defeat; it is death. It has a feeling of completeness to it, closely connected to smugness: the despairing person makes no attempt to move from the point he is at—no attempt to change himself or the world—and this completeness is a mark of dying. Dying is completion.

—Adin Steinsaltz

Most people see the problem of love as that of being loved, rather than that of loving, of one's capacity to love. Hence, the problem to them is how to be loved, how to be lovable. In pursuit of this aim, they follow several paths. One, which is especially used by men, is to be successful, to be as powerful and rich as the social

142

margin of one's position permits. Another, used especially by women, is to make oneself attractive, by cultivating one's body, dress, etc. Other ways of making oneself attractive, used both by men and women, are to develop pleasant manners, interesting conversation, to be helpful, modest, inoffensive. Many of the ways to make oneself lovable are the same as those used to make oneself successful, "to win friends and influence people." As a matter of fact, what most people in our culture mean by being lovable is essentially a mixture between being popular and having sex appeal.

—Eric Fromm
The Art Of Loving

There once was a king who was going to put to death many people, but before doing so he offered a challenge. If any of them could come up with something which would make him happy when he was sad, and sad when he was happy, he would spare their lives.

All night the wise men meditated on the matter.

In the morning, they brought the king a ring. The king said that he did not see how the ring would serve to make him happy when he was sad and sad when he was happy.

The wise men pointed to the inscription. When the king read it, he was so delighted that he spared them all.

And the inscription? "This too shall pass."

—Ram Dass
Journey Of Awakening

When action grows unprofitable, gather information; when information grows unprofitable, sleep.

—Ursula K. LeGuin
The Left Hand Of Darkness

○ ○ ○ ○ ○

We meet ourselves time and again in a thousand disguises on the path of life.

—Carl Jung

What I've found to be important is mainly just the realization that everyone has all knowledge and all humanity within themselves. Individual minds are connected to a universal mind. All people need to do is find out how to get it and reach it when they need it. Karma is simple truth: you reap what you sow.

—Willie Nelson

Religion is not any particular teaching. Religion is everywhere.

—Suzuki Roshi
Zen Mind, Beginner's Mind

To be an actor you've got to be honest. If you can fake that, you've got it made.

—George Burns

We work in the dark. We do what we can. We give what we have. Our doubt is our passion. Our passion is our task. The rest is the madness of art.

—Henry James

There is only one church and your membership is your belly button.

—Stephen Gaskin

Always do what's right. It will gratify half of mankind and astound the other.

—Mark Twain

Sometimes I worry about being a success in a mediocre world.

—Lily Tomlin

The average man seeks certainty in the eyes of the onlooker and calls that self-confidence. The warrior seeks impeccability in his own eyes and calls that humbleness.

—John Amodeo

I eat what I eat. Don't make eating complicated. Rules are made only when food is plentiful; in times of famine, one eats what one can get.

—Hari Dass

Storytelling reveals meaning without committing the error of defining it.

—Hannah Arendt

All sorrows can be borne if you put them into a story or tell a story about them.

—Isak Dinesen

You can't solve a problem on the same level that it was created. You have to rise above it to the next level.

—Albert Einstein

The bottom line is that (a) people are never perfect, but love can be, (b) that is the one and only way that the mediocre and the vile can be transformed, and (c) doing that makes it that. We waste time looking for the perfect lover, instead of creating the perfect love.

—Tom Robbins
Still Life With Woodpecker

Whoever loves true life, will love true love.

—Elizabeth Barrett Browning

It's a long old road, but I know I'm gonna find the end.

—Bessie Smith
"Long Old Road"

○ ○ ○ ○ ○

It is one of the commonest of mistakes to consider that the limit of our power of perception is also the limit of all there is to perceive.

—C. W. Leadbeater

Let us consider this waiter in the cafe. His movement is quick and forward, a little too precise, a little too rapid. He comes toward the patrons with a step a little too quick. He bends forward a little too eagerly; his voice, his eyes, express an interest a little too solicitous for the order of the customer. Finally there he returns, trying to imitate in his walk the inflexible stiffness of some kind of automaton while carrying his tray with the recklessness of a tight-rope walker by putting it in a perpetually unstable, perpetually broken equilibrium which he perpetually re-establishes by a light movement of the hand and arm. All his behavior seems to us

a game. He applies himself to chaining his movements as if they were mechanisms, the one regulating the other; his gestures and even his voice seem to be mechanisms; he gives himself the quickness and pitiless rapidity of things. He is playing; he is amusing himself. But what is he playing? We need not watch long before we can explain it: he is playing at *being* a waiter in a cafe.

—Jean-Paul Sartre
Being And Nothingness

The final belief is to believe in a fiction, which you know to be a fiction, there being nothing else. The exquisite truth is to know that it is a fiction and that you believe it willingly.

—Wallace Stevens

Were it possible for us to see further than our knowledge reaches, and yet a little way beyond the outworks of our divination, perhaps we would then endure our sorrows with greater confidence than our joys. For they are the moments when something new has entered us, something unknown; our feelings grow mute in shy perplexity, everything in us withdraws, a stillness comes, and the new, which no one knows, stands in the midst of it and is silent.

—Rainer Maria Rilke

If the only prayer you say in your whole life is "thank you," that would suffice.

—Meister Eckhart

One does not love a place less for having suffered in it.

—Jane Austen

From suffering I have learned this: that whoever is sore wounded by love will never be made whole unless she embraces the very same love which wounded her.

—Mechtild of Magdeburg

He only earns his freedom and existence who daily conquers them anew.

—Johann Wolfgang von Goethe

○ ○ ○ ○ ○

Draw your chair up close to the edge of the precipice and I'll tell you a story.

—F. Scott Fitzgerald
Notebooks

As long as we have some definite idea about or some hope in the future, we cannot really be serious with the moment that exists right now.

—Suzuki Roshi
Zen Mind, Beginner's Mind

Life is difficult. This is a great truth, one of the greatest truths. It is a great truth because once we truly see this truth, we transcend it. Once we truly know that life is difficult—once we truly understand and accept it—then life is no longer difficult. Because once it is accepted, the fact that life is difficult no longer matters.

—M. Scott Peck
The Road Less Traveled

I am alone with the beating of my heart.

—Lu Chi

Evil may be not seeing enough. So perhaps to become less evil we need only to see more.

—Corita

As the generation of leaves, so is that of men.

—Homer

Pleasure has desire in it. Desire is pain. There is no satisfaction. So pleasure is pain.

—Hari Dass

Attachment is a state of ignorance based on a memory of pleasure.

—Patañjali

The day I surrendered myself for God, I transcended all anxiety, because trying to look after oneself is the only anxiety.

—Bhagwan Shree Rajneesh

○ ○ ○ ○ ○

When you come right down to it all you have is yourself. The sun is a thousand rays in your belly. All the rest is nothing.

—Pablo Picasso

Like all young men I set out to be a genius, but mercifully laughter intervened.

—Laurence Durrell

It is good to have an end to journey toward; but it is the journey that matters, in the end.

—Ursula K. LeGuin
The Left Hand Of Darkness

Doubt is a pain too lonely to know that faith is his twin brother.

—Kahlil Gibran

What lies behind us and what lies before us are tiny matters compared to what lies within us.

—Ralph Waldo Emerson

If you think you are too small to be effective, you have never been in bed with a mosquito.

—Bette Reese

There is a story that as God and Satan were walking down the street one day, the Lord bent down and picked something up. He gazed at it glowing radiantly in His hand. Satan, curious, asked, "What's that?" "This," answered the Lord, "is Truth." "Here," replied Satan as he reached for it, "let me have that—I'll organize it for you."

—Ram Dass
Journey Of Awakening

When I marched with Martin Luther King in Selma, I felt my legs were praying.

—Rabbi Abraham Heschel

Analysis does not take into account the creative products of neurotic desires.

—Anaïs Nin

Slowly the earth will grow in the window. Blue she will gleam and brown and gray and silver and rose and red. Her clouds will cover her like curls of white hair, her clouds will turn dark as smoky pearls and the lavender of orchid, her clouds will be brown and green like marsh grass wet by the sea, and the sea will appear beneath

---

like pools of water in the marsh grass. The earth will look like a precious stone, blue as sapphire, blue as a diamond, the earth will be an eye to look at them in curious welcome as they return.
—Norman Mailer

The attainment of enlightenment from ego's point of view is extreme death, the death of self, the death of me and mine, the death of the watcher. It is the ultimate and final disappointment.
—Chögyam Trungpa
The Myth Of Freedom

I was not looking for my dreams to interpret my life, but rather for my life to interpret my dreams.
—Susan Sontag
The Benefactor

A certain Bektashi dervish was respected for his piety and appearance of virtue. Whenever anyone asked him how he had become so holy, he always answered, "I know what is in the Koran."

One day he had just given this reply to an enquirer in a coffeehouse, when an imbecile asked, "Well, what is in the Koran?"

"In the Koran," said the Bektashi, "there are two pressed flowers and a letter from my friend Abdullah."
—Idries Shah

"Why," a seventy-six-year-old woman was asked, "are you seeking therapy at your age?" Reflecting both her losses and her hopes, she answered, "Doctor, all I've got left is my future."
—Judith Viorst
Necessary Losses

Spend the afternoon. You can't take it with you.
—Annie Dillard

How [is one] to live a moral and compassionate existence when one is fully aware of the blood, the horror inherent in all life, when one finds darkness not only in one's culture but within oneself? If there is a stage at which an individual life becomes truly adult, it must be when one grasps the irony in its unfolding and accepts responsibility for a life lived in the midst of such paradox. One must live in the middle of contradiction because if all contradiction were eliminated at once life would collapse. There are simply no answers to some of the great pressing questions. You continue to live them out, making your life a worthy expression of leaning into the light.
—Barry Lopez
Arctic Dreams

We ate well and cheaply and drank well and cheaply and slept well and warm together and loved each other.
—Ernest Hemingway
A Moveable Feast

One cannot collect all the beautiful shells on the beach.
—Anne Morrow Lindbergh

SUNBEAMS

"What can't be said can't be said, and it can't be whistled either" are the words of someone whose identity perished several thousand years ago. They are for me a reflecting pool I return to again and again. At times I glimpse a shard of self whistling and I am strangely comforted, for what whistling is *not* in no way diminishes the sweet beauty of what it is.

—Hannah Carothers

A sheltered life can be a daring life as well. For all serious daring starts from within.

—Eudora Welty

Look everywhere with your eyes, but with your soul never look at many things, but at one.

—V.V. Rozinov

If you wait for tomorrow, tomorrow comes. If you don't wait for tomorrow, tomorrow comes.

—Senegalese proverb

All the way to heaven is heaven.

—St. Catherine of Siena

The service we render for others is really the rent we pay for our room on this earth.

—Wilfred Grenfell

You need not cry very loud. He is nearer to us than we think.

—Brother Lawrence

The mind cannot long act the role of the heart.

—François La Rochefoucauld

People seem not to see that their opinion of the world is also a confession of character.

—Ralph Waldo Emerson

The folly of mistaking a paradox for a discovery, a metaphor for a proof, a torrent of verbiage for a spring of capital truths, and oneself for an oracle is inborn in us.

—Paul Valéry

A poem . . . begins as a lump in the throat, a sense of wrong, a homesickness, a lovesickness. . . . It finds the thought and the thought finds the words.

—Robert Frost

The human face is really like one of those Oriental gods: a whole group of faces juxtaposed on different planes; it is impossible to see them all simultaneously.

—Marcel Proust

I have spent my days stringing and unstringing my instrument while the song I came to sing remains unsung.

—Rabindranath Tagore

○ ○ ○ ○ ○

Total freedom is never what one imagines and, in fact, hardly exists. It comes as a shock in life to learn that we usually only exchange one set of restrictions for another. The second set, however, is self-chosen, and therefore easier to accept.

—Anne Morrow Lindbergh

Fearful of separation, we repeat without remembering our history, imposing upon new sets, new actors, and a new production our unrecollected

but still-so-potent past. . . . No one is suggesting that we consciously remember experiences of early childhood loss, if by remember we mean that we can summon up a picture of mother leaving, of being alone in a crib. What stays with us instead is what it surely must have felt like to be powerless and needy and alone.

—Judith Viorst

The whole work of man really seems to consist in nothing but proving to himself every minute that he is a man and not a piano key.

—Fyodor Dostoyevsky

We must not allow other people's limited perceptions to define us.

—Virginia Satir

I only know myself as a human entity; the scene, so to speak, of thoughts and affections; and am sensible of a certain doubleness by which I can stand as remote from myself as from another. However intense my experience, I am conscious of the presence and criticism of a part of me, which, as it were, is not a part of me, but a spectator sharing no experience, but taking note of it, and that is no more I than it is you.

—Henry David Thoreau

I am a lie that always tells the truth.

—Jean Cocteau

It is better to know some of the questions than all of the answers.

—James Thurber

O O O O O

A poet looks at the world as a man looks at a woman.

—Wallace Stevens

She might struggle like a fly in a web. He wrapped her around and around with beautiful sentences.

—Mary Catherwood

Nobody can make you feel inferior without your consent.

—Eleanor Roosevelt

In real love you want the other person's good. In romantic love you want the other person.

—Margaret Anderson

No mockery in the world ever sounds to me as hollow as that of being told to *cultivate* happiness. . . . Happiness is not a potato, to be planted in mold, and tilled with manure.

—Charlotte Brontë

The trouble with being in the rat race is that even if you win, you're still a rat.

—Lily Tomlin

Wildness is the state of complete awareness. That's why we need it.

—Gary Snyder
Turtle Island

The best thing that can come with success is the knowledge that it is nothing to long for.

—Liv Ullmann
Changing

The enchanting, and sometimes terrifying, thing is that the world can be so many things to so many different souls. That it can be, and is, all these at once and the same time.

—Henry Miller
Big Sur, And The Oranges Of Hieronymus Bosch

To each other, we were as normal and nice as the smell of bread, we were just a family. In a family, even exaggerations make perfect sense.

—John Irving

Treat yourself at least as well as you treat other people.

—Theodore Rubin

There are two ways to slide easily through life: to believe everything or to doubt everything; both ways save us from thinking.

—Alfred Korzyski

Habit is habit, and not to be flung out of the window by any man, but coaxed downstairs a step at a time.

—Mark Twain
Puddinhead Wilson's Calendar

Discipline doesn't have to be about restriction, it can be about freedom, it can be about openness, it can be about more rather than less.

—Batya Zamir

My soul can find no staircase to heaven unless it be through earth's loveliness.

—Michelangelo

You know why newspapers are better than television? You can't swat flies with a TV.

—James Reed

○ ○ ○ ○ ○

"I learned one thing."

"What?"

"Never to go on trips with anyone you do not love."

—Ernest Hemingway
A Moveable Feast

. . . The more the soul knows, the more she loves, and loving much, she tastes much.

—St. Catherine of Siena

The finest sensibilities of the age are convulsed with pain. That means a change is at hand.

—Leonard Cohen

You must go on, I can't go on, I'll go on.

—Samuel Beckett

There is only one thing pain is good for. It teaches you to love. God bless pain.

—Joey Goldfarb

Dare we open our doors to the source of our being? What are flesh and bones for?

—Paul Reps

"It's a kind of test, Mary, and it's the only kind that amounts to anything. When something rotten like this happens, then you have your choice. You start to really be alive, or you start to die. That's all."

—James Agee
A Death In The Family

150

Those who justify themselves do not convince. To know truth one must get rid of knowledge; nothing is more powerful and creative than emptiness.

—Lao-tzu

There are numerous sidetracks which lead to a distorted ego-centered version of spirituality; we can deceive ourselves into thinking we are developing spiritually when instead we are strengthening our egocentricity through spiritual techniques.

—Chögyam Trungpa
Cutting Through Spiritual Materialism

I am myself plus my circumstance, and if I do not save it, I cannot save myself.

—José Ortega y Gasset

The power of memories and expectations is such that for most human beings the past and the future are not *as* real, but *more* real than the present.

—Alan Watts

Building a great tradition is more rewarding than simply having one.

—J.R. Slaughter

The vital democratic connection between community and leadership, between the mass and the several elites, has been so wrenched and perverted that disastrous policies go unchallenged time and again. . . .

—The Port Huron Statement, 1962
Students for a Democratic Society

There are no accidents whatsoever in the universe.

—Ram Dass

We've discovered that the earth isn't flat; that we won't fall off its edges, and our experience as a species has changed as a result. Maybe we'll soon find out that the self isn't "flat" either, and that death is as real and yet as deceptive as the horizon; that we don't fall out of life either.

—Seth
Jane Roberts' *Seth Speaks*

God glows and flames. . . . Eternity, believe it or not; it's as real as shit.

—Aldous Huxley
Island

Most of the shadows of this life are caused by standing in one's own sunshine.

—Ralph Waldo Emerson

○ ○ ○ ○ ○

The satiated man and the hungry one do not see the same thing when they look upon a loaf of bread.

—Jelaluddin Rumi

A wing is neither heaven nor earth.

—Antonio Porchia

The summation of all things is not God; it is man's limited perception of God.

—Ron Anjard

You have to sniff out joy, keep your nose to the joy-trail.

—Buffy Sainte-Marie

That's all nonviolence is—organized love.

—Joan Baez

Living had got to be such a habit with him that he couldn't conceive of any other condition.

—Flannery O'Connor

Because our goals are not lofty but illusory, our problems are not difficult, but nonsensical.

—Ludwig Wittgenstein

We must continuously discipline ourselves to remember how it felt the first moment.

—Sarah Caldwell

The truth will set you free. But before it does, it will make you angry.

—Jerry Joiner

Too much awareness, without accompanying experience, is a skeleton without the flesh of life.

—Anaïs Nin

○ ○ ○ ○ ○

How goes a life? Something like the ocean building dead coral.

—Stanley Moss

Tenderness contains an element of sadness. It is not the sadness of feeling sorry for yourself or feeling deprived but it is a natural situation of fullness. You feel so full and rich, as if you were about to shed tears. Your eyes are full of tears, and the moment you blink, the tears will spill out of your eyes and roll down your cheeks. In order to be a good warrior, one has to feel this sad and tender heart. If a person does not feel alone and sad, he cannot be a warrior at all.

—Chögyam Trungpa
Shambhala: The Sacred Path Of The Warrior

"I want the peace of God." To say these words is nothing. But to mean these words is everything. . . . No one can mean these words and not be healed. He cannot play with dreams, nor think he is himself a dream. He cannot make a hell and think it real. He wants the peace of God, and it is given him. For that is all he wants, and that is all he will receive. Many have said these words. But few indeed have meant them. You have but to look upon the world around you to be sure how very few they are.

—*A Course In Miracles*

Many we have worked with who were not in pain had less of a tendency to investigate, had less motivation to examine and begin to let go of their suffering. Because things weren't "so bad after all," they imagined they could somehow hide from death in the same way they had hidden from life.

—Stephen Levine
Who Dies?

The excursion is the same when you go looking for your sorrow as when you go looking for your joy.

—Eudora Welty

Of course there is nothing the matter with
    the stars
It is my emptiness among them
While they drift farther away in the invisible
    morning.

—W.S. Merwin
In The Winter Of My Thirty-Eighth Year

How simple and frugal a thing is happiness: a glass of wine, a roast chestnut, a wretched little brazier, the sound of the sea. . . . All that is required to feel that here and now is happiness, is a simple, frugal heart.

—Nikos Kazantzakis
Zorba The Greek

The face is masklike. It does not smile. It does not want to charm the mirror, or deceive the mirror, or flirt with it and gain a false answer. . . . You can never catch the face alive, laughing or loving.

—Anaïs Nin

The ring always believes that the finger lives for it.

—Malcolm de Chazal

All paths lead to the same goal: to convey to others what we are. And we must pass through solitude and difficulty, isolation and silence, in order to reach forth to the enchanted place where we can dance our clumsy dance and sing our sorrowful song—but in this dance or in this song there are fulfilled the most ancient rites of our conscience in the awareness of being human and of believing in a common destiny.

—Pablo Neruda

The melody is in the eyes.

—Nicholas Ray

What is this darkness? What is its name? Call it: an aptitude for sensitivity. Call it: a rich sensitivity which will make you whole. Call it: your potential for vulnerability.

—Meister Eckhart

The Blues is the truth. You'd better believe that what they're telling you is the truth.

—Buddy Guy

When mind soars in pursuit of the things conceived in space, it pursues emptiness. But when the man dives deep within himself, he experiences the fullness of existence.

—Meher Baba

It's all soul.

—Junior Wells

The truth which makes us free is not an absolute ideal but truthfulness.

—Evan Thomas

Gentle and giving—all the rest is treason.

—Kenneth Patchen

Man becomes great exactly in the degree to which he works for the welfare of his fellow men.

—Mahatma Gandhi

Love thy neighbor, even when he plays the trombone.

—Jewish proverb

Don't admire wavy hair when your date wears a crew cut.

—Kathryn Murray
Tips To Teen-Agers

I have decided to stick with love. Hate is too great a burden to bear.

—Martin Luther King, Jr.

How charming was, and is, the chanciness of being a girl. One has a kind of honey. But not for bees. You walk into a drawing room and a dark man or a light man or a red man may change your life for no reason. . . .

You might think that a woman of seventy-eight, glancing at a house where she was once in love, would be full of regrets. The extraordinary thing about age is that you don't regret love.

Even in the looking glass there's nothing to be done. The golden veil has blown off the face.

It isn't that I was what's called, rather unhandsomely, "highly sexed." But it was such a surprise that one could attract. It was like a stream finding out that it could move a rock. The pleasure of one's effect on other people still exists in age—what's called making a hit. But the hit is much rarer and made of different stuff.

—Enid Bagnold
Autobiography

In the evening of our lives we shall be examined in love.

—St. John of the Cross

Conduct is more convincing than language.

—John Woolman

I learned to trust my obsessions. It is surely a great calamity for a human being to have no obsessions.

—Robert Bly

Oh, for the wonder
that bubbles into my soul.

—D.H. Lawrence

We have not even to risk the adventure alone, for the heroes of all time have gone before us; the labyrinth is thoroughly known: we have only to follow the thread of the hero path. And where we had thought to find an abomination, we shall find a god: where we had thought to slay another, we shall slay ourselves; where we had thought to travel outward, we shall come to the center of our own existence; and where we had thought to be alone, we shall be with all the world.

—Joseph Campbell

○ ○ ○ ○ ○

He who knows that enough is enough will always have enough.

—Lao-tzu
Tao Te Ching

There is no place to seek the mind;
It is like the footprints of the birds in the sky.

—Zenrin
The Gospel According To Zen

The teaching which is written on paper is not the true teaching. Written teaching is a kind of food for your brain. Of course it is necessary to take some food for your brain, but it is more important to be yourself by practicing the right way of life.

—Suzuki Roshi
Zen Mind, Beginner's Mind

We tend to think of the rational as a higher order, but it is the emotional that marks our lives. One often learns more from ten days of agony than from ten years of contentment.

—Merle Shain
Some Men Are More Perfect Than Others

Your duty is to be; and not to be this or that.

—Ramana Maharshi

Sometime we shall have to stop overevaluating the word. We shall learn to realize that it is only one of the many bridges that connect the island of our soul with the great continent of common life . . . the broadest, perhaps, but in no way the most refined.

—Rainer Maria Rilke

Somewhere, and I can't find where, I read about an Eskimo hunter who asked the local missionary priest, "If I did not know about God and sin, would I go to hell?" "No," said the priest, "not if you did not know." "Then why," asked the Eskimo earnestly, "did you tell me?"

—Annie Dillard
Pilgrim At Tinker Creek

It is not that you must be free from fear. The moment you try to free yourself from fear, you create a resistance against fear. Resistance, in any form, does not end fear. What is needed, rather than running away or controlling or suppressing or any other resistance, is understanding fear; that means, watch it, learn about it, come directly into contact with it. We are to learn about fear, not how to escape from it, not how to resist it through courage and so on.

—J. Krishnamurti

A young lad was sent to school. He began his lessons with the other children, and the first lesson the teacher set him was the straight line, the figure "one." But whereas the others went on progressing, this child continued writing the same figure. After two or three days the teacher came up to him and said, "Have you finished your lesson?" He said, "No, I'm still writing 'one.' " He went on doing the same thing, and when at the end of the week the teacher asked him again he said, "I have not yet finished it." The teacher thought he was an idiot and should be sent away, as he could not or did not want to learn. At home the child continued with the same exercise and the parents also became tired and disgusted. He simply said, "I have not yet learned it, I am learning it. When I have finished I shall take the other lessons." The parents said, "The other children are going on further, school has given you up, and you do not show any progress; we are tired of you." And the lad thought with sad heart that as he had displeased his parents, too, he had better leave home. So he went into the wilderness and lived on fruits and nuts. After a long time he returned to his old school. And when he saw the teacher he said to him, "I think I have learned it. See if I have. Shall I write on this wall?" And when he made his sign the wall split in two.

—Hazrat Inayat Khan
The Sufi Message Of Hazrat Inayat Khan

○ ○ ○ ○ ○

Selfishness is not living as one wishes to live; it is asking others to live as one wishes to live.

—Oscar Wilde

If there is anything that we wish to change in the child, we should first examine it and see whether it is not something that could better be changed in ourselves.

—Carl Jung

Successful marriage is always a triangle: a man, a woman, and God.

—Cecil Myers

Lovers, children, heroes, none of them do we fantasize as extravagantly as we fantasize our parents.

—Francine du Plessix Gray

Jesus' "lack of moral principles." He sat at meals with publicans and sinners, he consorted with harlots. Did he do this to obtain their votes? Or did he think that, perhaps, he could convert them by such "appeasement"? Or was his humanity rich and deep enough to make contact, even in them, with that in human nature which is common to all men, indestructible, and upon which the future has to be built?

—Dag Hammarskjöld
Markings

There is one spectacle grander than the sea,
That is the sky;
There is one spectacle grander than the sky,
That is the interior of the soul.

—Victor Hugo

We cannot become saints merely by trying to run away from material things.

—Thomas Merton

Great men, like nature, use simple language.

—Luc de Clapiers Vauvenargues

The Buddhas and the Christs that we know are but second-rate heroes in comparison with the greatest men of whom the world knows nothing. Hundreds of these unknown heroes have lived in every country working silently. Silently they live and silently they pass away; and in time their thoughts find expression in Buddhas or Christs, and it is these latter that become known to us. The highest men do not seek to get any name or fame from their knowledge. They leave their ideas to the world; they put forth no claims for themselves and establish no schools or systems in their name. Their whole nature shrinks from such a thing. They are the pure Sattvikas, who can never make any stir, but only melt down in love. . . . The highest

156

kind of men silently collects true and noble ideas, and others—the Buddhas and Christs—go from place to place preaching them and working for them. In the life of Gautama Buddha we notice him constantly saying that he is the twenty-fifth Buddha. The twenty-four before him are unknown to history, although the Buddha known to history must have built upon foundations laid by them. The highest men are calm, silent, and unknown. They are the men who really know the power of thought; they are sure that, even if they go into a cave and close the door and simply think five true thoughts and then pass away, these five thoughts of theirs will live through eternity. Indeed such thoughts will penetrate through the mountains, cross the oceans, and travel through the world. They will enter deep into human hearts and brains and raise up men and women who will give them practical expression in the workings of human life.

—Swami Vivekananda
Karma Yoga

○ ○ ○ ○ ○

After taking ninety-nine years to climb a stairway, the tortoise falls and says there is a curse on haste.

—Maltese proverb

I have called this center the self. Intellectually, the self is no more than a psychological concept, a construct that serves to express an unknowable essence, which we cannot grasp as such, since by definition it transcends our powers of comprehension. It might equally be called

"the God within us." . . . The self has as much to do with the ego as the sun with the earth.

—Carl Jung

Mysteries are not necessarily miracles.

—Johann Wolfgang von Goethe

Shallow men believe in luck, believe in circumstance. Strong men believe in cause and effect.

—Ralph Waldo Emerson

I perhaps owe having become a painter to flowers.

—Claude Monet

The majority of people are subjective toward themselves and objective toward all others, terribly objective sometimes, but the real task is, in fact, to be objective toward oneself and subjective toward all others.

—Sören Kierkegaard

My love is my weight.

—St. Augustine

How could I have expected that after a long life I would understand no more than to wake up at night and to repeat: strange, strange, strange, O how strange, how strange, O how funny and strange.

—Czeslaw Milosz

The barb in the arrow of childhood suffering is this: its intense loneliness, its intense ignorance.

—Olive Shriner

157

They always told me when I was young, "Just wait, and you'll see." Now I'm old and see nothing. It's wonderful.

—Eric Satie

You do not realize your own situation. You are in prison. All you can wish for, if you are a sensible man, is to escape. But how to escape? . . . If a man is at any time to have a chance of escape, then he must first of all realize that he is in prison. So long as he fails to realize this, so long as he thinks he is free, he has no chance whatsoever.

—G.I. Gurdjieff

In the Highlands of New Guinea I saw men with photographs of themselves mounted on their foreheads so they would be recognized.

—Ted Carpenter

We do not succeed in changing things according to our desire, but gradually our desire changes. The situation that we hoped to change because it was intolerable becomes unimportant. We have not managed to surmount the obstacle, as we were absolutely determined to do, but life has taken us around it, led us past it, and then if we turn around to gaze at the remote past, we can barely catch sight of it, so imperceptible has it become.

—Marcel Proust

As though naturally erasers would speak the language of pencils.

—Howard Nemerov

That sudden and ill-timed love affair may be compared to this: you take boys somewhere for a walk; the walk is jolly and interesting—and suddenly one of them gorges himself with oil paint.

—Anton Chekhov

There is sanctuary in reading, sanctuary in formal society, in the company of old friends, and in the giving of officious help to strangers, but there is no sanctuary in one bed from the memory of another.

—Cyril Connolly

Perfect love means to love the one through whom one became unhappy.

—Sören Kierkegaard

People who have not been in Narnia sometimes think that a thing cannot be good and terrible at the same time.

—C.S. Lewis

There are two kinds of faithfulness in love: one is based on forever finding new things to love in the loved one; the other is based on our pride in being faithful.

—François La Rochefoucauld

A man too good for the world is no good for his wife.

—Yiddish proverb

Love matches, as they are called, have illusion for their father and need for their mother.

—Friedrich Nietzsche

One writes of scars healed, a loose parallel to the pathology of the skin, but there is no such thing in the life of an individual. There are open wounds, shrunk sometimes to the size of a pinprick, but wounds still. The marks of suffering are more comparable to the loss of a finger or the sight of an eye. We may not miss them, either, for one minute in a year, but if we should there is nothing to be done about it.
—F. Scott Fitzgerald
Tender Is The Night

There is a palace that opens only to tears.
—*Zohar*

They were lovely, your eyes, but you didn't know where to look.
—George Seferis

○ ○ ○ ○ ○

Whatever authority I may have rests solely on knowing how little I know.
—Socrates

Marvelous Truth, confront us
at every turn
in every guise
—Denise Levertov

If you want to write the truth, you must write about yourself. I am the only real truth I know.
—Jean Rhys

People try to get out of themselves and to escape from the man. This is folly; instead of transform-ing themselves into angels, they turn themselves into beasts; instead of lifting, they degrade themselves. These transcendental humors frighten me, like lofty and inaccessible heights.
—Michel de Montaigne

Were it possible for us to wait for ourselves to come into the room, not many of us would find our hearts breaking into flower as we heard the door handle turn.
—Rebecca West

Men are so willing to respect anything that bores them.
—Marilyn Monroe

Martyrdom . . . is the negation of any spiritual value, because martyrdom is suffering turned in on the self in glamour and glorification for what a person is going through.
—David Spangler

Forget about likes and dislikes. They are of no consequence. Just do what must be done. This may not be happiness, but it is greatness.
—George Bernard Shaw

Though clear waters range to the vast blue
autumn sky,
How can they compare with the hazy moon on
a spring night!
Most people want to have pure clarity,
But sweep as you will, you cannot empty the
mind.
—Keizan Zenji

Eighty percent of life is just showing up.
—Woody Allen